Freud for the Twenty-First Century

"With this nimble volume, Samuels emerges as a peerless Freudian life coach. Without ever abandoning Freud's own belief in the value of science, and engaging with key contemporary advocates of the enlightenment doctrine, he articulates the so desperately needed, poetic wisdom for our times. This is a book to be read and re-read, *ad infinitum*."

—Dany Nobus, *Brunel University London*

Robert Samuels

Freud for the Twenty-First Century

The Science of Everyday Life

Robert Samuels
University of California, Santa Barbara
Santa Barbara, CA, USA

ISBN 978-3-030-24381-4   ISBN 978-3-030-24382-1   (eBook)
https://doi.org/10.1007/978-3-030-24382-1

This Palgrave Pivot imprint is published by the registered company Springer Nature Switzerland AG
The registered company address is: Gewerbestrasse 11, 6330 Cham, Switzerland

CONTENTS

CHAPTER 1

Introduction: The Science of Everyday Life

Abstract This chapter argues that Freud's theories and practices can help us live better lives by applying the scientific method to everyday life. Although Freud resisted giving advice, and he focused on abnormal psychology, my goal is to show that we can take his ideas and apply them to how we understand our selves and the world around us in the twenty-first century. Not only can we live more rational and satisfying lives, but we can also overcome many of our political and social problems if we understand how reason, emotions, desires, and the unconscious work.

Keywords Freud · Science · Reason · Emotion · Desire · Unconscious

In this book, I argue that Freud's theories and practices can help us live better lives by applying the scientific method to everyday life. Although Freud resisted giving advice, and he focused on abnormal psychology, my goal is to show that we can take his ideas and apply them to how we understand our selves and the world around us in the twenty-first century. Not only can we live more rational and satisfying lives, but we can also overcome many of our political and social problems if we understand how reason, emotions, desires, and the unconscious work.

The first step in this process is to define the scientific process and how Freud applies it to everyday life. As I discuss in Chapter 2, on its most basic level, modern science seeks to use reason to judge reality by first

© The Author(s) 2019
R. Samuels, *Freud for the Twenty-First Century*,
https://doi.org/10.1007/978-3-030-24382-1_1

eliminating all preconceived notions and then testing ideas against the reactions of empirical reality. For Freud, the goal of analysis was to help people apply this scientific method to their perceptions of their own lives and the world around them. On the most fundamental level, Freud examined why it was so hard for people to abide by what he called the "reality principle," and much of his work examines the different ways people escape from the reality of their lives.[1]

In Chapter 3, I turn to Freud's misunderstood theory of the pleasure principle to examine why people are driven to remove themselves from tension and conflict by repressing their own sense of guilt, shame, responsibility, and freedom. Freud posits that the core drive of human beings is to use as little energy as possible by avoiding all stimulation, and this type of psychic death leads to lives dominated by addiction and makes it difficult for us to address important interpersonal and social problems. In fact, I argue that the biggest threat facing humanity is our ability to derive instant pleasure from new technologies, media, and drugs.

As I describe in Chapter 4, our mental freedom from reality should be seen as both a positive and negative thing. On a positive side, imagination helps us to consider alternative ways of thinking and living, but this freedom from material reality can also lead us to escape from seeing the truth of our world and our own actions. Freud called this alternative to reality the primary processes, and he stressed how the human mind is often shaped by irrational fantasies.[2] Moreover, Freud insisted that infants naturally hallucinate the satisfaction of their wishes, and so they have to be taught to differentiate between their internal fantasies and external reality. I claim in this chapter that the primary way that people escape reality and satisfy the demands of the pleasure principle is through wish fulfillment in the unconscious.

In Chapter 5, I discuss how Freud's theory of transference and narcissism relate to the way that we make a call to others to fix reality and help us satisfy the pleasure principle. Not only do we turn to others to satisfy our desires, but we want our others to verify our sense of being good and right. Moreover, this structure of obsessional narcissism helps to explain the limitations of contemporary liberalism and the failure of many forms of analysis and therapy.

In Chapter 6, I examine some of the many ways that people misunderstand psychoanalysis and global progress. In reviewing the distorted interpretations of the pleasure principle, the reality principle, the primary processes, and transference, I reveal how psychoanalysis has been repressed from within psychoanalysis itself. I also connect this repression to the ways people deny the evidence concerning our global progress. The final chapter looks at Yuval Harari's *21 Lessons for the 21st Century* to examine why liberal academic culture often rejects global progress and focuses on negative portrayals of the world. By using Freud's fundamental concepts to analyze Harari's work, I provide a model for psychoanalytic cultural criticism. The goal then of this work is to show that psychoanalysis is not only still relevant today, but in actuality, Freud's theories and practices have never been more essential for understanding and changing ourselves and the world around us.

NOTES

1. Freud develops his ideas on the reality principle in "Project for a scientific psychology (1950 [1895])." *The Standard Edition of the Complete Psychological Works of Sigmund Freud, Volume I (1886–1899): Pre-Psycho-Analytic Publications and Unpublished Drafts.* 1966. 281–391; and "Formulations on the two principles of mental functioning." *The Standard Edition of the Complete Psychological Works of Sigmund Freud, Volume XII (1911–1913): The Case of Schreber, Papers on Technique and Other Works.* 1958. 213–226.
2. Hilgard, Ernest R. "Impulsive versus realistic thinking: An examination of the distinction between primary and secondary processes in thought." *Psychological Bulletin* 59.6 (1962): 477.

CHAPTER 2

Science and the Reality Principle

Abstract This chapter reveals how on the most basic level, modern science seeks to use reason to judge reality by first eliminating all preconceived notions and then testing ideas against the reactions of empirical reality. For Freud, the goal of analysis was to help people apply this scientific method to their perceptions of their own lives and the world around them. On the most fundamental level, Freud examined why it was so hard for people to abide by what he called the "reality principle," and much of his work examines the different ways people escape from the reality of their lives.

Keywords Science · Freud · Reality principle · Pinker · Enlightenment

In his book *Totem and Taboo*, Freud argues that there have been three major stages in human history, and each one is dominated by a different belief system. At first, people believed that everything had a spiritual existence (animism), and they did not differentiate between their thoughts and reality.[1] Then a transition was made to religion, where people asked a divine power that they created to answer their prayers. Finally in the third modern period of science, the main change is that people give up on the omnipotence of their own ideas. This is an interesting way of thinking about science because Freud does not say that science

© The Author(s) 2019
R. Samuels, *Freud for the Twenty-First Century*,
https://doi.org/10.1007/978-3-030-24382-1_2

shows the power of our knowledge; instead he argues that with science, we acknowledge the limitations of our own thoughts.[2]

A fundamental aspect, then, of applying science to everyday life is to humbly accept that our understanding of our selves and our world is limited, and so we must not think that we know everything already. In fact, when Freud discusses the development of his own thought, he often stresses how his knowledge is a work in progress and that a scientist has to always be open to discarding ideas when reality reveals a different truth.[3] Just as Descartes begins his scientific method with doubt and skepticism, we should be willing to put into question our current knowledge in order to be open to discover something new.[4] Part of this process relies on critical introspection because we need to acknowledge and then eliminate our prejudices and assumptions. Of course this is easier said than done, but the modern world of science and reason begins with this necessary but impossible goal of total impartiality. In fact, our democratic legal system also relies on the ideal of having an impartial judge who weighs evidence in an open way without prejudice. From this perspective, modern science and democracy share many of the same ideals and principles, and when we apply these ideals to everyday life, we are trying to look at the world and our selves from an impartial perspective as we apply the reality principle to judge empirical evidence.

THE REALITY PRINCIPLE AND GLOBAL PROGRESS

As Steven Pinker has documented in his book *Enlightenment Now*, this combination of reason, modern science, and democracy has led to a world where on average, people live longer, healthier, freer, and happier lives than they ever did before.[5] In fact, global life expectancy has doubled in the last 150 years, and much of this is due to science, reason, education, and democratic law. As Pinker highlights, we have also witnessed a period of increased human rights and a reduction of violent deaths; even though most people are not aware of these improvements. Some of the main global advances Pinker documents are the following:

1. Over the last two hundred years, the rate of global extreme poverty has gone from 90 to 10%, and close to half of the reduction has occurred during the last 35 years (87);
2. There are now 103 democracies in the world representing 53% of the global population (203);

3. During the last thirty years, 66% of all countries have stopped using capital punishment (209);
4. In 1950, close to half of the nations in the world had laws discriminating against ethnic or racial minorities. In 2003, that number went down to less than 20% (323);
5. In 1900, New Zealand was the only country that allowed women to vote; now, they can vote in every country except the Vatican City. Also, 40% of the labor force is now female and 20% of the members of national parliaments are women make up almost 40% of the labor force worldwide and more than a fifth of the members of national parliaments (222).
6. "The World Opinion Poll and Pew Global Attitudes Project have each found that more than 85 percent of their respondents believe in full equality for men and women, with rates ranging from 60 percent in India, to 88 percent in six Muslim-majority countries, to 98 percent in Mexico and the United Kingdom" (222);
7. "The world's literacy rate doubled in the next century and quadrupled in the century after that, so now 83 percent of the world is literate" (236);
8. "In 1919, an average American wage earner had to work 1800 hours to pay for a refrigerator; in 2014, he or she had to work fewer than 24 hours (and the new fridge was frost-free and came with an icemaker)" (251);
9. "The proportion of people killed annually in wars is less than a quarter of what it was in the 1980s, a seventh of what it was in the early 1970s, an eighteenth of what it was in the early 1950s, and a half a percent of what it was during World War II" (158);
10. "Laws that criminalize homosexuality continue to be stricken down, and attitudes toward minorities, women, and gay people are becoming steadily more tolerant, particularly among the young, a portent of the world's future. Hate crimes, violence against women, and the victimization of children are all in long-term decline, as is the exploitation of children for their labor" (221).

These tremendous advances, which many people take for granted, have all been enabled by the use of reason in science, law, government, and technological development. From this global perspective, the reality principle, in the form of impartial reason, has made our lives on average healthier, wealthier, longer, and freer.

Therefore, the application of science to everyday life not only helps us to live a more effective and lasting life, but it also helps to make the world a better place. Although we do not know all of the causes and effects of this global progress, we do know that on average, as people become more educated and less reliant on religion and other tradition-based belief systems, they become wealthier, healthier, and freer.[6] There is thus a parallel between the way science affects us as individuals and the way it affects the world in general.[7]

FREUD, SCIENCE, AND THE REALITY PRINCIPLE

When individuals stop relying on religion and other imaginary belief systems to determine how they see themselves and reality, they can turn to science, reason, and education. Unfortunately, there are always resistances to this transition, and people tend to cling to unreason, emotion, and intuition.[8] In fact, Freud's concepts of the pleasure principle, the primary processes, and transference help us to see why it is so hard to take a scientific perspective on our own lives. Since we do not want to acknowledge anything that will cause tension or conflict, we tend to turn to our imagination and create an alternative reality in our heads.[9]

Paradoxically, since science forces us to accept the limitations of our own knowledge, it clears the path for us to learn new knowledge, but each time we learn something new, we have to give up old knowledge, which had been a source of pleasure and stability. Due to the fact that Freud saw science as not only the main alternative to religion but also the key to the reality principle, he combined individual analysis with social analysis.[10] In other words, individual development and historical development follow the same path.

What is so interesting is that even though Freud always considered himself to be a scientist, his theories and practices have been rejected as being non-scientific. Critics argue that Freud has no empirical evidence backing up his ideas, and his work did not engage in traditional empirical experimentation.[11] However, I claim that the opposite is the case because Freud constantly applied the main principles of the scientific method, which rely on the impartial observation of empirical evidence.

THE METHOD OF ANALYSIS

Many people now argue that it is impossible to be impartial and neutral, and the very idea of neutrality represents a hidden bias.[12] However, we need to think of neutrality as a bias against bias, and as a necessary but impossible ideal, it is something that we strive to attain even though we never fully get there. In the case of the practice of psychoanalysis, Freud stumbled upon the notion that the best way to get patients to say whatever is on their minds is for the analyst to remain neutral in regards to the content and meaning of what the patient says. Neutrality and free association are therefore closely linked, and they represent the key innovations of psychoanalytic practice.[13]

Guiding Freud's method is the underlying idea that it is impossible for a person to completely erase a memory, thought, or feeling. The goal of analytic treatment is, then, to use free association to discover all of the important memory-thoughts that have been repressed or denied. However, the biggest obstacle to this approach is that due to the pleasure principle, people do not want to say or think about anything that makes them look bad in front of others and their own self. Analysis thus has to find a way to suspend the critical conscience of the patient, and the main way it does this is by removing the analyst from the position of social censor or judge.

By accident, Freud realized that if he did not sit right in front of his patients, they were more likely to engage in the process of free association. The reason for this effect is that our social conscience is in part derived from being subjected to the look of others. Since we do not know what other people are thinking, we assume that when they look at us, they are judging our actions; the psychoanalytic method, then, tries to suspend the social censor in order to get people to speak without self-censorship. It turns out that free association is not very easy to do, but it is the only path to the approach of reality and truth in analysis. Free association trains people to suspend their own prejudices and self-interest so that they can become impartial witnesses to their own minds and lives.

WHY THERE IS NO SELF-ANALYSIS

The relation between neutrality and free association also help us to understand why it is impossible to completely analyze yourself. While one part of the process of analysis is self-discovery, the other part involves training yourself to ignore the presence of the other person. In fact, people often report today that their biggest fear is public speaking, and one reason why they have this fear is that they constantly imagine that other people are judging them negatively.[14] I know from personal experience that one of the great benefits of my own analysis was my increased ability to speak in front of other people without any anxiety.

Since we never know what the analyst is thinking, we are able to examine all of the different ways we project our own fears and desires onto others, and this is only possible if there is another real person in the room. As we shall see in a later chapter on transference, a key to analytic treatment is overcoming the narcissistic structure where we place others in a position to only be able to verify our good self. This type of idealizing transference has to be worked through in analysis so that we learn how to stop trying to get our ideal self recognized by an idealized other.[15]

The presence of the analyst is also necessary because much of the treatment deals with discovering the way our demands posed to other people are based on childhood desires for unconditional love, recognition, and knowledge.[16] Since the analyst is present, but does not fulfill the demands of the patient, the source of the patient's requests eventually become clarified. It is simply impossible to work through these issues on your own, and so self-analysis is ultimately impossible, but we can still use psychoanalytic principles to live a better life and help promote a better world.

TRUTH AND ANALYSIS

Perhaps the most essential idea driving Freud's theories and practices is his argument that a memory can never be completely erased. In other words, we cannot escape our own truth and reality because our memories are always maintained somewhere in our minds. As Lacan argues, Freud's certainty and ethical approach is based on this theory of truth.[17] Since the repressed always returns and the truth will eventually bare its ugly head, the key is to provide a situation where this emergence of truth will re-appear. Eventually, Freud found that by letting his patients say whatever came to their minds without censorship, they would discover the reality and truth of their own thoughts and perceptions.[18] Like an impartial scientist, one is trained to follow the evidence wherever it leads, and to do this, one has to suspend one's own presuppositions and prejudices.

Not only did Freud believe that memories could not be completely lost for good, but he also believed that all memories are linked together in a network of associations, and therefore, it is possible to discover repressed memories by following the paths of the associations. As a neurologist, Freud also believed that neurons are also linked in the same way, and so his theory of memory is also a theory of neural connections.[19] From this perspective, there is little difference between memories and neurons, and in fact, both of these concepts are related to how language functions. In all three cases—memories, neurons, and words—one element is linked to another element, and it is this linking system that provides the framework for Freud's understanding of the unconscious and free association.[20]

Once Freud gave up on the practice of hypnotizing his patients and suggesting to them their missing memories and thoughts, he realized that people can discover their own buried truth if they are given the opportunity to follow the path of their own thoughts without censorship.[21] The trick here was to get people to speak about so many different but related things that they would stumble across something that they did not intend to say. By simply following the chain of associations of different memories and ideas, Freud was able to discover something new, and this new entity, he called the unconscious. Moreover, he realized that people often avoided the truth of their own circumstances and history by refusing to say everything that was on their mind, yet Freud also found that these same people could not escape the truth because they did not have total control over their own ideas.[22]

To understand this notion of free association and the network of mental association, all you have to do is to pay attention to your own thoughts, and soon you will see that you usually do not control the path of your own thinking. One idea leads to another, and we often cannot predict where these ideas will lead.[23] The sense that we control our thinking through our intentions is just an illusion generated by what Freud calls secondary revision, and if we are really honest with ourselves, we have to admit that thoughts move in unpredictable and uncontrollable ways. Furthermore, we spend a great deal of time trying to get in control of our wandering thoughts by imposing some type of order after the fact. Just as scientists are supposed to follow truth by going wherever it take us, true free association means that we follow our thoughts no matter where they go.

One of Freud's related insights connected to this idea of free association is the notion that even though we do not control our own thoughts, these linked ideas do follow a logical path that can be re-traced and examined.[24] The way, then, that we inspect our own minds in a scientific way is to follow the connections between our associated ideas. Since we know that every word is defined in relation to other words, every memory gains its meaning in relation to other memories, and this creation of meaning is dependent on how these different entities (neurons, memories, thoughts, and words) are connected.

The next stage in understanding how this science of the mind works is to realize that just as poetry uses the substitution and association of disconnected symbols to create new ideas, our minds have the automatic ability to link together seemingly unrelated things through the process of substitution and displacement.[25] For instance, when you see your uncle Joe in your dream, he is really a symbol for a set of feelings and memories and not just your uncle. In fact, everything in your dream is a symbol or metaphor, and just as one symbol is used to represent another symbol, the feelings that belong to one memory are displaced onto another memory.[26] The best way to figure all of this out is to write down everything you remember about your dreams, and then allow your mind to free associate on each dream element so that you retrace the different displacements and substitutions of your mind.[27]

It may seem that we have gotten away from our original goal of applying the scientific method to our own lives, but if you really want to understand yourself, you have to see how the unconscious is structured and how you can learn about your own thinking through the process of free association.

SCIENCE VS. SCIENTISM

Although the main argument of this book is that you can apply the scientific method to your own everyday life, you also have to recognize the limits of scientific thinking. In fact, as Freud argues, science begins with the acknowledgement of the limits of our own thoughts to fully grasp reality, and so the best we can do is to constantly strive to picture a better approximation of the truth. When scientists fail to recognize their limits, they engage in what is now called scientism, which is the belief that science already has the answers to all of our questions.[28]

In the next chapter, we shall see how this quest to apply the scientific method to everyday life is undermined by the pleasure principle. Not only do we often try to escape all tension and conflict to maintain the lowest level of mental energy, but the way we reduce anxiety is by ignoring the reality of our own memories and experiences. This constant attempt to escape from reality and responsibility entails a repression of feelings of guilt and shame; however, these attempts ultimately fail, and the repressed always returns in some way.[29]

NOTES

1. Freud, Sigmund. *Totem and Taboo: Some Points of Agreement Between the Mental Lives of Savages and Neurotics*. Routledge, 2013.
2. "If we accept the evolution of man's conceptions of the universe mentioned above, according to which the *animistic* phase is *succeeded* by the *religious*, and this in turn by the *scientific*, we have no difficulty in following the fortunes of the 'omnipotence of thought' through all these phases. In the animistic stage man ascribes omnipotence to himself; in the religious he has ceded it to the gods, but without seriously giving it up, for he reserves to himself the right to control the gods by influencing them in some way or other in the interest of his wishes. In the scientific attitude towards life there is no longer any room for man's omnipotence; he has acknowledged his smallness and has submitted to death as to all other natural necessities in a spirit of resignation. Nevertheless, in our reliance upon the power of the human spirit which copes with the laws of reality, there still lives on a fragment of this primitive belief in the omnipotence of thought" (*Totem* 116).
3. "We have often heard it maintained that sciences should be built up on clear and sharply defined basic concepts. In actual fact no science, not even the most exact, begins with such definitions. The true beginning of scientific activity consists rather in describing phenomena and then in proceeding to group, classify and correlate them. Even at the stage of description it is not possible to avoid applying certain abstract ideas to the material in hand, ideas derived from somewhere or other but certainly not from the new observations alone. Such ideas—which will later become the basic concepts of the science—are still more indispensable asthe material is further worked over. They must at first necessarily possess some degree of indefiniteness; there can be no question of any clear delimitation of their content. So long as they remain in this condition, we come to an understanding about their meaning by making repeated references to the material of observation from which they appear to have been derived, but upon which, in fact, they have been imposed. Thus, strictly speaking, they are in the nature of conventions—although everything depends on their not being arbitrarily chosen but determined by their having significant relations to the empirical material, relations that we seem to sense before we can clearly recognize and demonstrate them. It

is only after more thorough investigation of the field of observation that we are able to formulate its basic scientific concepts with increased precision, and progressively so to modify them that they become serviceable and consistent over a wide area. Then, indeed, the time may have come to confine them in definitions. The advance of knowledge, however, does not tolerate any rigidity even in definitions. Physics furnishes an excellent illustration of the way in which even 'basic concepts' that have been established in the form of definitions are constantly being altered in their content." Freud, Sigmund. "Instincts and their vicissitudes." *The Standard Edition of the Complete Psychological Works of Sigmund Freud, Volume XIV (1914–1916): On the History of the Psycho-Analytic Movement, Papers on Metapsychology and Other Works.* 1957. 109–140.

4. Descartes, René. *A Discourse on Method.* Vol. 3. Prabhat Prakashan, 1969.
5. Pinker, Steven. *Enlightenment Now: The Case for Reason, Science, Humanism, and Progress.* Penguin Books, 2019.
6. Wilkinson, Richard and Kate Pickett. *The Spirit Level: Why Equality Is Better for Everyone.* Penguin Books, 2010.
7. Li, Liman Man Wai and Michael Harris Bond. "Value change: Analyzing national change in citizen secularism across four time periods in the World Values Survey." *The Social Science Journal* 47.2 (2010): 294–306.
8. Handy, Charles. *The Age of Unreason.* Random House, 2012.
9. Freud's theory of the conflict between the reality principle and the pleasure principle is articulated in "Formulations on the two principles of mental functioning." *The Standard Edition of the Complete Psychological Works of Sigmund Freud, Volume XII (1911–1913): The Case of Schreber, Papers on Technique and Other Works.* 1958. 213–226.
10. "Animism, the first conception of the world which man succeeded in evolving, was therefore psychological. It did not yet require any science to establish it, for science sets in only after we have realized that we do not know the world and that we must therefore seek means of getting to know it" (*Totem* 140).
11. Crews, Frederick. "The verdict on Freud." *Psychological Science* 7.2 (1996): 63–68.
12. Fausto-Sterling, Anne. "The myth of neutrality: Race, sex and class in science." *The Radical Teacher* (1981): 21–25.
13. Freud, Sigmund. "Remembering, repeating and working-through (Further recommendations on the technique of psycho-analysis II)." *The Standard Edition of the Complete Psychological Works of Sigmund Freud, Volume XII (1911–1913): The Case of Schreber, Papers on Technique and Other Works.* 1958. 145–156.
14. Blöte, Anke W., et al. "The relation between public speaking anxiety and social anxiety: A review." *Journal of Anxiety Disorders* 23.3 (2009): 305–313.

15. Lacan, Jacques. *The Seminar of Jacques Lacan: Book 2: The Ego in Freud's Theory and in the Technique of Psychoanalysis 1954–1955*. CUP Archive, 1988.
16. Lacan, Jacques. "The seminar of Jacques Lacan: Book V: The formations of the unconscious: 1957–1958." (2011).
17. Lacan, Jacques. *The Four Fundamental Concepts of Psycho-analysis*. Vol. 11. W. W. Norton, 1998.
18. Freud, Sigmund. "Remembering, repeating and working-through (Further recommendations on the technique of psycho-analysis II)." *The Standard Edition of the Complete Psychological Works of Sigmund Freud, Volume XII (1911–1913): The Case of Schreber, Papers on Technique and Other Works*. 1958. 145–156.
19. "We can then assert that *memory is represented by the facilitations existing between the neurones*. It is therefore more correct to say that memory is represented by the *differences* in the facilitations between the neurons" (Project).
20. In his Project for a Scientific Psychology, Freud clearly anticipates both structural linguistics and contemporary neuroscience: "Every neuron must in general be presumed to have several paths of connection with other neurons -that is, several contact-barriers. It is on this that the possibility depends of the excitation having a choice of path, determined by facilitation. This being so, it is quite clear that the condition of facilitation of each contact-barrier must be independent of that of all the others in the same neuron. Otherwise there would once again be no possibility of one path being preferred to another-no motive, that is."
21. Kris, Anton O. *Free Association: Methods and Process*. Routledge, 2013.
22. Freud, Sigmund. "Repression." *The Psychoanalytic Review (1913–1957)* 9 (1922): 444.
23. Baird, Benjamin, et al. "Inspired by distraction: Mind wandering facilitates creative incubation." *Psychological Science* 23.10 (2012): 1117–1122.
24. The logic of the unconscious is explained in the following passage from Freud's Project: "Our consciousness of dream ideas is above all a discontinuous one. It does not become aware of a whole chain of associations but only of separate points in it; and between them lie unconscious intermediate links which we can easily discover when we are awake. If we investigate the reasons for these leaps, here is what we find. Suppose that *A* is a dream-idea that has become conscious and that it leads to *B*. But, instead of *B*, *C* appears in consciousness and it does so because' it lies on the path between *B* and another cathexis *D*, which is simultaneously present. Thus there is a diversion owing to a simultaneous cathexis of another kind, which is not, moreover, conscious. *C* has therefore taken the place

of *B*, though *B* fits in better with the chain of thought, that is, with the wish-fulfilment" (Project 403).

25. Freud first develops his theory of the interpretation of dreams and the unconscious in his Project: "For instance, [I have a dream that] O. has given Irma an injection of propyl I then see 'trimethylamin' very vividly before me, and hallucinate its formula *[C]*. The thought that is simultaneously present is of Irma's illness being of a sexual nature *[D]*. Between this thought and that of propyl lies an association *[B]* of a conversation on sexual chemistry with W. Fl. [Wilhelm Fliess] in which he drew my special attention to trimethylamin. This latter idea is then pushed into consciousness from both directions. It is a puzzling fact that neither the intermediate link (sexual chemistry *[B]*) nor the diversionary idea (the sexual nature of the illness *[D]*) are also conscious. And this needs explaining. One might suppose that the cathexis of B or D alone would not be intense enough to bring about a retrogressive hallucination, but that C, being cathected from both of them, would be able to do so" (Project 403).

26. "The fact that memory of the wishful idea is kept cathected, all the while the chain of association is followed from neurone *c*. As we know, the fact of the cathexis of neurone *b* will increase the facilitation and accessibility of any connections it may have" (Project 392).

27. Freud, Sigmund. "The handling of dream-interpretation in psycho-analysis." *The Standard Edition of the Complete Psychological Works of Sigmund Freud, Volume XII (1911–1913): The Case of Schreber, Papers on Technique and Other Works*. 1958. 89–96.

28. Sorell, Tom. *Scientism: Philosophy and the Infatuation with Science.* Routledge, 2013.

29. Freud, Sigmund. "Repression." *The Standard Edition of the Complete Psychological Works of Sigmund Freud, Volume XIV (1914–1916): On the History of the Psycho-Analytic Movement, Papers on Metapsychology and Other Works*. 1957. 141–158.

CHAPTER 3

The Pleasure Principle and the Death Drive

Abstract This chapter examines Freud's misunderstood theory of the pleasure principle to analyze why people are driven to remove themselves from tension and conflict by repressing their own sense of guilt, shame, responsibility, and freedom. Freud posits that the core drive of human beings is to use as little energy as possible by avoiding all stimulation, and this type of psychic death leads to lives dominated by addiction and makes it difficult for us to address important interpersonal and social problems. In fact, I argue that the biggest threat facing humanity is our ability to derive instant pleasure from new technologies, media, and drugs.

Keywords Pleasure principle · Freud · Drugs · Virtual reality · Repression

Much of Freud's essential theories and insights are first developed in his early, unpublished *Project for a Scientific Psychology.*[1] In this groundbreaking work, we are given the fundamental relationship among the reality principle, the pleasure principle, the primary processes, and transference. The basic system Freud articulates is the following: (1) the pleasure principle pushes us to avoid all tension and conflict, but we cannot escape from our internal desires; (2) the first method of escape is the primary processes in the form of hallucinating the object of desire; (3) when hallucination fails to remove tension, the child cries in order to get the parent to fix reality and return the child to a state of pleasure; and (4) when all else fails, the child is forced to accept the reality of non-satisfaction. The vast majority of Freud's theories all relate to this fundamental structure.[2]

UNDERSTANDING PLEASURE

To comprehend the pleasure principle, we can look at the main arguments from the *Project*, which have been rarely understood. For Freud, the primary driving force of all human subjectivity is defined by a law of mental inertia, which is first presented as a law of mental physics: "What I have in mind is *the principle of neuronic inertia*, which asserts that neurones tend to divest themselves of quantity ... Reflex movement now becomes intelligible as an established method of thus getting rid of quantity. The principle of inertia provides the reason for reflex movement" (357). Freud uses here a physical model of stimulus and release in order to argue that as humans, we are driven to escape from excitement, tension, and stimulation. Later on in his work, he equates the pleasure principle with what he calls the death drive because the goal of life is to ultimately eliminate all energy.[3] It is vital to stress here that the pleasure principle and the death drive are not mythical, mystical, or mysterious; rather they represent a general physical law of mental activity.

Freud insists that just as the primary goal of the physical body is to release energy and tension, the neural system also is determined by this same law of inertia: "This process of discharge is the primary function of neuronic systems" (357). From this perspective, our minds and brains are shaped by a set of processes dedicated to reducing tension and creating a state of homeostatic order. Moreover, this primary function of the pleasure principle is coupled with the tendency of flight in the face of threatening stimuli: "At this point there is an opportunity for the development of a *secondary* function. For among the various methods of discharge those are preferred and retained which involve a cessation of the *stimulus-i.e., flight* from the stimulus. A balance is observed here between the quantity of the excitation and the effort required for flight from that stimulus; so that the principle of inertia is not disturbed in this case" (357). The idea here is not only that we seek to avoid tension and conflict, but that we escape in a way that does not require the use of too much effort and energy.

Using a model of brain activity based on the organization of neurons in a network of association, Freud posits that the pleasure principle is equated with the system of perception, but this system has to remain an open system with no permanent traces: "We cannot, however, attribute this characteristic to the vehicles of consciousness. The mutability of their content, the transitoriness of consciousness, the easy combination of simultaneously perceived qualities-all these tally only with complete permeability of the perceptual neurones coupled with full *restitutio in integrum* [return to their former state]" (371).[4] As Freud will argue in *Beyond the Pleasure Principle*, the death drive represents a move back to an original inorganic state, and here this compulsion to return to a state of nothingness is equated with the need for consciousness to always be open to new perceptions.[5] The subject is defined in this theory as an empty and open receiver of information, or in Lacanian terms, the subject is a void or a hole.[6]

THE PLEASURE PRINCIPLE IN OUR DAILY LIVES

A key take away from Freud's theory of the pleasure principle is that our main mental drive is to avoid tension, and this process involves fleeing from reality. We can see this form of the death drive occurring in many different aspects of contemporary life. One obvious example is the way that people turn to drugs in order to remove themselves from feelings of anxiety, guilt, and shame. From this psychoanalytic perspective, addiction involves denying the difficult realities of one's life; however, we know that these inner and outer realities never go away, and so addictions eventually fail to accomplish their goals.

One way that people do try to overcome their addictions is by going to Alcoholics Anonymous (AA) and other similar groups.[7] As a form of "wild analysis," these organizations often try to get people to admit their shame and guilt, but they also often affirm that addiction is a disease, and one must surrender to a higher power.[8] In my later chapter on transference, I will explain how this type of surrendering personal responsibility is counter-productive, but what I want to focus on here is the way that the disease narrative serves to further enhance the pleasure principle and the death drive.

Although many people have been helped by AA, the idea that people have an incurable disease may serve to remove them from a sense of responsibility and freedom, and this avoidance of responsibility reinforces the pleasure principle's drive to escape from anxiety, guilt, and shame. Therefore, even when people are told to examine their past behavior and address their own sense of guilt and shame, the disease narrative eliminates the role of individual choices since people can always say that the disease made them act in a certain way. What we find here is a partial cure that often leads to a displacement of addictions through the use of tobacco, caffeine, and other substances.[9] As drug addiction continues to be a major personal and social problem in our world, we have to realize that treatment will not be successful if it only serves to reinforce the death drive in the form of the pleasure principle.

VIRTUAL PLEASURE

Perhaps even more threatening to our species than drug addiction is the way that people turn to media technologies in order to gain instant access to pleasure. As our technologies get better at simulating reality, people are motivated to ignore the real world and retreat into a virtual world.[10] For instance, I once asked a student why she constantly used her phone in class, and she said that she takes out this device whenever she feels uncomfortable.[11] Her phone therefore functioned to provide pleasure by removing her from an anxiety-producing social world. In fact, if you walk around a college campus, you will see most of the students either texting, phoning, or listening to music, and this compulsive use of media technologies not only can cut them off from the external world around them, but it distracts them from their own self-reflection.

An interesting analysis of this type of media addiction occurs in the film *The Matrix*, where the character Morpheus offers the main character, Neo, a choice between two pills. One pill will allow him to live in a fantasy world of pleasure, and the other pill will allow him to unplug and enter into what is called the "desert of the real." The main character picks reality, but we experience this choice through a media production, and so we are still part of the pleasure principle. In fact, in a key seen, Morpheus tells Neo that people do not want to unplug from the media because it gives them such easy access to pleasure.

Humans have therefore built technologies and cultural products that enable the pleasure principle to rule our lives, and the question becomes how do we learn to unplug from this system? One reason why I feel this question is so important is that we will not even try to fix existential problems like climate change if we are constantly denying the reality of our lives, and with the increased ubiquity and effectiveness of virtual media, this problem will only get worse. Just as pornography allows people to escape from the difficulties and tensions of real relationships, virtual reality is an accepted form of denying the reality principle.

MISUNDERSTANDING PLEASURE

One of my hopes is that this chapter will help to correct the way pleasure is represented in psychoanalytic theory and the broader culture. People think that pleasure means the pure pursuit of enjoyment and excitement, but the opposite is actually the truth. The pleasure principle is self-destructive because it is directed towards eliminating tension, excitement, and ultimately reality. Although some people think that the goal of psychoanalysis is the pursuit of happiness, what I have been showing is that this pursuit is actually the enactment of a self-destructive death drive.

In *Beyond the Pleasure Principle*, Freud introduces this notion of the death drive by describing a game he witnessed his grandson playing.[12] This child tied a reel of cotton to a string, and he would play at throwing it away from him and then pulling it back. Freud hypothesized that the child was trying to overcome the separation of his parents by replacing them with the symbolic reel that he could now control. Freud also noticed that when the child threw the object away, he would make a sound representing the word "gone," and when he pulled it back, he would make the sound for the word "here." The French psychoanalyst Jacques Lacan argued that the child was using language and symbolization to make an absent object present and a present object absent.[13] The game, and language in general, thus, gave the child the ability to escape from reality and overcome the anxiety of separation from his parents. In this case, the death drive and the pleasure principle were enacted through language, symbolization, and culture. Moreover, in a footnote, Freud added that the child would also play at making his own self appear and disappear by looking at himself in the mirror and then ducking down so he was no longer reflected.[14]

When the child not only replaces his parents but also effaces himself, we see how language and culture give us access to the pleasure principle by denying the presence of our selves and others in an effort to escape tension and anxiety. A destructive aspect of culture therefore entails an escape from reality, the self, and others. What psychoanalysis, then, offers is a theory and practice for reducing our reliance on the pleasure principle as we learn to accept the tension and conflicts of reality and our own minds.

THE BRIBE OF ENJOYMENT

Another important discovery Freud made in relation to the pleasure principle was his realization that one of the main functions of jokes is an implicit deal made between the joke teller and the audience where the speaker gives the audience pleasure, and in response, they agree not to criticize the content of the joke.[15] Freud articulates here a key aspect of popular culture, which is the exchange between what he called the bribe of enjoyment and the criticism of the other. In short, people are able to express their repressed aggression and sexual desire in a hidden way by using indirect language, and in this structure, the pleasure principle is realized by removing the subject from criticism, shame, guilt, and responsibility.

An interesting case of this exchange can be seen in the work of Slavoj Zizek who often combines serious philosophy with jokes and references to popular culture.[16] What Zizek does not seem to realize is that his performance relies on giving his audience pleasure so that they do not hold him morally responsible for what he says. In other words, jokes allow him and his audience to activate the pleasure principle and to repress the super-ego and the reality-testing ego.

This interplay between the unconscious and the pleasure principle is one of the defining aspects of contemporary culture and media capitalism. In fact, the way that society often gets people to accept unequal and exploitative relationships is by bribing people with pleasure. Within this structure, cultural systems render people passive and apathetic by creating the illusion of freedom, realness, and pleasure. For instance, many libertarian politicians present the fantasy of a free market in order to cater to people's desire to be free from social restraint. Underlying this fantasy structure is the idea that freedom is the ultimate form of pleasure, and this pleasure can free one from feelings of guilt, shame, and responsibility.

This social use of the pleasure principle can be seen in the literary critic Mikhail Bakhtin concept of the carnivalesque, which explores how societies often create festivals where there is a temporary suspension of moral rules and social hierarchies.[17] One of Bakhtin's underlying assumptions is that people will accept their daily exploitation if they are occasionally given an escape through pleasure. From this perspective, what often blocks the reality principle and the discovery of the truth of one's situation and the system that oppresses them is a temporary bribe of enjoyment. There thus can be no real social or personal progress if we simply use pleasure to escape from reality.

Liberal Racism

Not only do people use popular culture to realize the goals of the death drive and the pleasure principle, but they also use the escape from criticism in order to project aggression and sexuality onto other people in a safe and hidden way. A great example of this system can be found in the movie *Get Out!* While we are used to thinking of racism as a conservative ideology, what this film reveals is the way that liberal popular culture allows people a safe way to both idealize and devalue other people, especially people of color. In the plot of the film, a white liberal neuroscientist has organized a system where black men are kidnapped and hypnotized, and later the brains of old white people are transplanted into the black bodies. On one level, the idea here is that white people idealize the physical and sexual prowess of black males, but they do not value their minds, and so they want to combine their white minds with black bodies. However, on another level, the film is clearly about the ways the media acts as a form of hypnosis that renders its audience passive consumers of self-destructive messages. In other words, the media not only idealizes and devalues black men, but it also robs them of their ability to fight back.

The underlying theme of the movie can be understood through the psychoanalytic theories of projection, identification, hypnosis, and the pleasure principle. In liberal racism, the dominant culture projects its own repressed sexual and aggressive desires onto other people who are both idealized and devalued. These others who receive the projected desires internalize them in a form of self-hatred and social assimilation. However, a key aspect of this cultural fantasy is the idea that the other has been able to escape civilization's renunciations, and so unlike the members of the dominant class, the dark other is able to experience sex and violence without guilt, shame, or inhibition. In this process of idealizing the pleasure of the other, the dominant group can identify with the one who escapes from social restrictions, and yet this other also represents a threat because they are not controlled by civilizing forces.

If one looks at popular television shows and mainstream movies, they mostly all present the fantasy of idealized and devalued others who are able to freely realize the pleasure principle without any social inhibitions. These idealize others allow us to activate our own pleasure principles through a process of identification, and the result is that we are able to experience sex and violence without any sense of guilt, shame, anxiety, or responsibility. On a fundamental level, fictional productions always come with an ethical escape clause, which implicitly states that no one is responsible for what is said and done; after all, it is just a fiction, or a joke, or a character, or a fantasy. Fictional culture therefore functions by realizing the pleasure principle and repressing reality.

In the next chapter, I explain Freud's theory of the primary processes and the unconscious as they relate to the pleasure principle and the repression of the reality principle. We shall see that the primary processes in the unconscious are focused on the imaginary fulfillment of desire, and this internal mechanism frees people from dealing with the reality of the external and internal worlds.

NOTES

1. Kris, Ernst (Eds.). *The Origins of Psycho-Analysis: Letters to Wilhelm Fliess, Drafts and Notes, 1887–1902* (James Strachey, Trans.). London: Imago, 1954. 347–445; A project for a scientific psychology. *SE*, 1: 283–387.
2. In Lacan's *Four Fundamental Concepts of Psychoanalysis*, he argues that Freud's four main concepts are the unconscious, repetition, drives, and transference. My book modifies Lacan's interpretation but is based in part on the same key theories in Freud's work. Lacan, Jacques. *The Four Fundamental Concepts of Psycho-Analysis*. Vol. 11. W. W. Norton, 1998.
3. Freud, Sigmund. *Beyond the Pleasure Principle*. Penguin Books, 2003.
4. For Freud's further articulation of the relation between memory, consciousness, and perception, see Freud, Sigmund. "A note upon the 'mystic writing-pad'." *The Standard Edition of the Complete Psychological Works of Sigmund Freud, Volume XIX (1923–1925): The Ego and the Id and Other Works*. 1961. 225–232.
5. Freud, Sigmund. *Beyond the Pleasure Principle*. Penguin Books, 2003.
6. Lacan, *Four*, 20–28.
7. Kurtz, Ernest. "Why AA works: The intellectual significance of Alcoholics Anonymous." *Journal of Studies on Alcohol* 43.1 (1982): 38–80.

8. Freud, Sigmund. "'Wild' psycho-analysis." *The Standard Edition of the Complete Psychological Works of Sigmund Freud, Volume XI (1910): Five Lectures on Psycho-Analysis, Leonardo da Vinci and Other Works.* 1957. 219–228.
9. Galaif, Elisha R. and Steve Sussman. "For whom does Alcoholics Anonymous work?" *International Journal of the Addictions* 30.2 (1995): 161–184.
10. Harari, Yuval Noah. *Homo Deus: A Brief History of Tomorrow.* Random House, 2016.
11. Song, Indeok, et al. "Internet gratifications and Internet addiction: On the uses and abuses of new media." *Cyberpsychology & Behavior* 7.4 (2004): 384–394.
12. Freud, *Beyond*, 15.
13. Lacan, *Four*, 62, 239.
14. Freud, *Beyond*, 16, n.1.
15. Freud, Sigmund. *Jokes and Their Relation to the Unconscious.* W. W. Norton, 1960.
16. Žižek, Slavoj. *Žižek's Jokes: (Did You Hear the one About Hegel and Negation?).* MIT Press, 2014.
17. Webb, Darren. "Bakhtin at the seaside: Utopia, modernity and the carnivalesque." *Theory, Culture & Society* 22.3 (2005): 121–138.

CHAPTER 4

The Unconscious and the Primary Processes

Abstract This chapter explains why our mental freedom from reality should be seen as both a positive and negative thing. On a positive side, imagination helps us to consider alternative ways of thinking and living, but this freedom from material reality can also lead us to escape from seeing the truth of our world and our own actions. Freud called this alternative to reality the primary processes, and he stressed how the human mind is often shaped by irrational fantasies. Moreover, Freud insisted that infants naturally hallucinate the satisfaction of their wishes, and so they have to be taught to differentiate between their internal fantasies and external reality. I claim in this chapter that the primary way that people escape reality and satisfy the demands of the pleasure principle is through wish fulfillment in the unconscious.

Keywords Unconscious · Primary processes · Freud · Hallucination · Fantasy

In the last chapter, I examined how people are able to escape from reality by using drugs and media technologies to accomplish the goals of the pleasure principle, which is to avoid all tension and conflict. What I want to now articulate is the way that the pleasure principle can avoid the reality principle through an internal mechanism, which Freud calls wish fulfillment. Therefore without turning to external media or drugs, the unconscious is able to satisfy itself and escape from its need to adjust to

R. Samuels, *Freud for the Twenty-First Century*,
https://doi.org/10.1007/978-3-030-24382-1_4

27

reality. From this perspective, the primary processes in the unconscious represent one of the biggest threats to global progress and personal well-being because this mental capacity for self-satisfaction eliminates the need to test reality and approach life and others from a perspective of neutral impartiality.

THE PRIMARY PROCESSES IN THE UNCONSCIOUS

In *The Project for a Scientific Psychology*, Freud argues that the pleasure principle is temporarily disrupted when a child encounters an internal need that is not satisfied: "From the very first, however, the principle of inertia is upset by another set of circumstances. As the internal complexity of the organism increases, the neuronic system receives stimuli from the somatic element itself-endogenous stimuli, which call equally for discharge. These have their origin in the cells of the body and give rise to the major needs: hunger, respiration and sexuality. The organism cannot withdraw itself from them as it does from external stimuli."[1] Freud will later calls these unmet needs "wishes" or "desires," and he will claim that the main function of the unconscious is to fulfill wishes by imagining the presence of previous scenes of satisfaction.[2]

For Freud, the first way that the child fulfills these wishes is through the process of hallucination: "Wishful cathexis carried to the point of hallucination and a complete generation of unpleasure, involving a complete expenditure of defence, may be described as 'psychical primary processes'" (388). From this perspective, the primary processes are defense mechanisms that function through the process of hallucination, which in turn, satisfies the goal of the pleasure principle. Freud also connects the primary processes to the state of dreaming and the formation of the unconscious: "In the waking state this store is collected in the 'ego', and we may assume that it is the discharging of the ego which is the precondition and characteristic of sleep. And here, we can see at once, we have the precondition of primary psychical processes" (398). Freud argues here that it is the ego that is put to sleep in the dream state, and this negation of the self allows for the regression to the primary processes. In other words, the unconscious is rendered possible through this double process of eliminating the ego and generating a hallucination: "Sleep is characterized by motor paralysis, a paralysis of the will" (399). We should therefore define the unconscious by the negation of the will and the realization of the pleasure principle through the hallucination of a wish fulfillment.

In the *Project*, Freud posits that one of the things that makes the unconscious dream state possible is the fact that at night, one separates from the system of perception-consciousness: "It is a highly interesting fact that the state of sleep begins and is evoked by the closing of those sense organs that are capable of being closed. Perceptions should not be made during sleep and nothing disturbs sleep more than the emergence of sense impressions" (399). Just as the ego must be put out of action, external stimuli need to be eliminated in order to allow for the emergence of the unconscious and the primary processes. Freud adds that we find many of these same conditions in the event of hypnosis: "At this point, too, we might approach the enigma of hypnosis. The apparent unexcitability of the sense organs in that condition would seem to rest on this withdrawal of the cathexis of attention" (399). By introducing the hypnotic relation into his definition of the primary process, Freud reveals a fundamental connection between social influence and the unconscious. As he emphasizes here, in both the dream state and the hypnotic relation, the will becomes paralyzed. The incredible leap Freud makes should not be missed because we begin to see how he developed his theory of the unconscious out of a double experience of interpreting dreams and using hypnosis. Moreover, if we want to understand why people will submit to an ideology or leader without critical analysis or reality testing, we have to understand how primary processes work in the unconscious.

As Freud continues to define the primary process through his description of dreams and other unconscious phenomenon, we see how he offers an alternative model to how our minds work: "The connections in dreams are partly nonsensical, partly feeble-minded or even meaningless or strangely demented. The last of these attributes is explained by the fact that the compulsion to associate prevails in dreams, as no doubt it does primarily in all psychical life. Two cathexes that are simultaneously present must, so it seems, be brought into connection with each other" (400). This passage is key because it shows that at the heart of all human thought is a compulsion to associate unrelated experiences. Although it appears that Freud is first only speaking about an abnormal condition, he quickly adds that he considers this primary process to be a part of "all psychical life." Unconscious primary processes are therefore at the foundation of all thought.

If Freud's claim about the unconscious foundation of thinking seems absurd or new, we should remember that just before Descartes announces his famous, "I think, therefore, I am," he relates how he is unable to distinguish between the dream state and the waking state: "considering that all the same thoughts which we have when awake can also come to us when we are asleep, without there being truth in any of them at the time, I determined to pretend that everything which had ever entered my mind was no more true than the illusions of my dreams. But immediately afterwards I noticed that, while I wished in this way to think everything was false, it was necessary that I—who was doing the thinking—had to be something. Noticing that this truth—I think; therefore, I am—was so firm and so sure that all the most extravagant assumptions of the sceptics would not be able to weaken it, I judged that I could accept it without scruple as the first principle of the philosophy I was looking for."[3] While Descartes turns to the dream state in order to insist that his ego or "I" remains certain in both the true world and the false world, Freud realizes that the ego is effaced in the dream and that this lack of intention not only defines the unconscious but all thought. In other words, we only imagine that we control our thoughts, but the linking of our ideas does not require conscious intention. Moreover, as Descartes highlights, on the level of pure thought, we cannot distinguish the fictional dream state from the real world. In other words, the unconscious means that human beings are able to break with material reality through a form of mental autonomy, but they are not in control of their own thinking.

At the start of his *Discourse on Method*, Descartes defines reason as the ability to distinguish truth from fiction, but as we saw above, on the level of pure thought, this distinction is lost, and so reason and the reality principle are set aside by the primary processes. Once again, this sacrifice of reality testing and the putting to sleep of the ego are not purely pathological events because they define the very core of our thinking. Not only do we hallucinate in a psychotic way each night when we dream, but whenever we think about something, we are prone to activate the pleasure principle by imagining the fulfilment of our wishes. In Lacan's words, our approach to the world is shaped by desire and the irrational and unintentional association of ideas.[4]

Once Freud establishes the unconscious nature of the primary process, he then moves from the internal dream state to the external world of social relations: "I have collected some amusing examples of the dominance of this compulsion in waking life (For instance, some provincial spectators who were present in the French Chamber during a bomb outrage concluded that whenever a deputy made a successful speech a shot was fired as a sign of applause.)" (400). Here Freud points to his future work on the psychopathology of everyday life by indicating that unconscious primary processes also occur throughout our waking life. Whenever we make a connection between two unrelated events or representations, we are utilizing the primary processes to realize the wish of creating order and therefore reducing tension.

Although Freud does signal continuity between the unconscious state and everyday mental functioning, he also seeks to distinguish between the two: "Ideas in dreams are of a hallucinatory nature; they awaken consciousness and meet with belief. This is the most important characteristic of dreams. It becomes obvious at once in alternate fits of sleeping and waking. One shuts one's eyes and hallucinates, one opens them and thinks in words" (401). What then distinguishes unconscious thinking from "normal" mental functioning is that when one is awake, one mediates one's thoughts through words and is open to new perceptions, and yet, Freud also wants to insist that the recalling of our memories entails hallucination: "we might turn back to the nature of the primary process and point out that the primary recollection of a perception is always a hallucination and that it is only inhibition on the part of the ego which has taught us never to cathect... in such a way that it can transfer cathexis retrogressively ..." (401). From this radical perspective, our primal tendency to hallucinate the recollection of past perceptions has to be prevented by an ego that inhibits the process of regression. In other words, the reality principle has to intervene through the ego in order to prevent the primary processes from realizing the goals of the pleasure principle.[5]

As he continues to detail the unconscious primary processes, Freud focuses on the underlying cause of fulfilling desires through hallucination: "The purpose and meaning of dreams (or at least of normal ones) can be established with certainty. Dreams are *the fulfilments of wishes*-that is, primary processes following on experiences of satisfaction; and they are not recognized as such, merely because the release of pleasure (the reproduction of pleasurable discharges) in them is slight, since in general they run their course almost without affect (*i.e.*, without motor release). But it is very easy to prove that this is their nature. And it is for this very reason that I am inclined to infer that *primary wishful cathexes too are of a hallucinatory character*" (402). This theory of the hallucination of the fulfillment of a wish in the unconscious will push Freud to argue in *The Interpretation of Dreams* that dreams represent a psychosis of short duration. Furthermore, in *Totem and Taboo*, he posits that the first stage of human collective life is determined by the same primary process through the notion of animism.[6] In both the dream state and the animistic culture, internal mental associations are experienced as an outer perception. Thus, on a fundamental level, the primary processes entail that thoughts in the unconscious are experienced as external perceptions; moreover, these thoughts are based on memories of past experiences and the fulfillment of unmet needs.

The unconscious is thus a defensive structure that evades the reality testing of the ego and experiences the satisfaction of wishes by treating memories as if they are external objects. From this perspective, we are all insane because our thinking circumvents the reality principle. Yet, we shall see that this madness is contained and inhibited by being repressed into a state of unawareness.

EMOTIONS AND NEUROSIS

In another bold move that has been rarely noticed or understood, Freud compares affects to the unconscious primary processes: "In a word, the affective process approximates to the uninhibited primary process" (415). From a psychoanalytic viewpoint, emotions are derived from our mental ability to project thoughts onto reality and confuse memories with perceptions. It will then be the task of the reality principle to develop a method to distinguish internal memories from external perceptions. Moreover, Freud shows that the problem with some emotions is that they avoid reality testing by fulfilling desires through the process of confusing memories with perceptions.

It is important to point out that Freud equates dreams with psychosis and animistic cultures because he finds in all three structures the same tendency to confuse internal thoughts with external reality; however, his next move is to show how we are all affected by these primary processes in the unconscious, but unlike psychotics, we are simply unaware of our own mental functioning. The reason for this lack of awareness relies on how we are able to displace and replace unconscious thoughts with conscious intentions. Freud first works out this relationship in the *Project* by examining obsessional and hysterical neurotics: "If, when dreams are remembered, we enquire from consciousness as to their content, we shall find that the meaning of dreams as wishfulfilments is concealed by a number of processes all of which we meet with once more in the neuroses and which are characteristic of the pathological nature of those disorders" (402). Just as most people say they cannot remember their dreams or they do not dream at all, neurotics utilize a series of defense mechanisms called secondary revision to conceal the content of their unconscious.[7]

The first way that the contents of the unconscious are hidden is by the separation of the underlying desire from the manifest content: "We shall not find, for instance, a wish that is conscious and afterwards its fulfilment hallucinated; but the latter only will be conscious and the intermediate link [the wish] will have to be inferred" (404). Freud posits that we are not aware of our own desires, and all that we can remember is the fulfillment of our wishes. It is precisely this separation of the manifest expression of the unconscious and the latent desire that pushes Lacan to turn to the linguistic distinction between the signifier and the signified. On the most basic level, this theory tells us that we may know the signs and words we use, but the underlying desire and meaning is hidden.[8]

Freud first worked out this theory of the primary processes by analyzing his own dreams and talking to hysterical patients who showed up in his office with symptoms that could not be explained through medical anatomy or psychological understanding. These patients' symptoms represented a break with natural anatomy and mental continuity, and he explains this break by outlining the unconscious primary processes: "Every observer of hysteria is at once struck by the fact that hysterical patients are subject to a *compulsion*, which is operated by means of *excessively intense ideas*. An idea may emerge into consciousness with special frequency, without the course of events justifying it; or it may be that the arousing of this neurone is accompanied by psychical consequences which are unintelligible. The emergence of the excessively intense idea has results which, on the one hand, cannot be suppressed and, on the other hand, cannot be understood: releases of affect, motor innervations, inhibitions. The subject is by no means without insight into the strangeness of the situation" (405). Freud posits here that the hysterical patients knew that something irrational was happening, but they could not explain the cause or the meaning of their symptoms, which often expressed themselves in inappropriate emotions and uncontrollable, incomprehensible, intense thoughts.

Before he tries to explain how hysterical thinking works, he sums of the experience of their symptoms in the following manner: "Thus hysterical compulsion is (1) incomprehensible; (2) incapable of being cleared up by any process of thought, and (3) incongruous in its structure" (405–406). In other words, hysterics are plagued by thoughts and feelings that they can neither understand nor control. To further clarify this structure, Freud distinguishes between "normal" emotional reactions and the responses of hysterics: "For instance, suppose a man runs into danger by being thrown out of a carriage and that afterwards driving in a carriage becomes impossible for him. Such a compulsion is (1) comprehensible, since we know its origin; and (3) not incongruous, since the association with danger makes it justifiable to link driving in a carriage with fear. It, too, however, is incapable of being cleared up by any process of thought. This last characteristic cannot be described as entirely pathological; our *normal* excessively intense ideas as well are often incapable of being cleared up. One would be inclined to regard neurotic compulsions as completely non-pathological, if it were not that experience shows that a compulsion of this kind in a normal person only persists for a short time after its occasion, and then disintegrates by degrees. Thus the persistence of a compulsion is pathological and points to a *simple neurosis*" (406). What then distinguishes the hysterical reaction to a bad event from the normal reaction is the persistence of the compulsion to think about the event and respond emotionally. This explanation of emotions and compulsive thoughts means that affects are often the result of displaced emotions derived from repressed memories, and what makes emotion pathological is when the intensity of the feelings does not dissipate over time.

THE MENTAL NETWORK

The question is now why do these compulsions last so long for neurotics, and how can they be resolved. To begin to answer this problem, Freud sees the mind as a network of associations that function by linking one idea, neuron, memory, thought and feeling to another, and pathology enters into the picture when one of the associations is either replaced or lost: "*Before* the analysis, *A* is an excessively intense idea, which forces its way into consciousness too often, and each time it does so leads to tears. The subject does not know why *A* makes him weep and regards it as absurd - but he cannot prevent it. *After* the analysis, it has been discovered that there is an idea *B* which rightly leads to tears and which rightly recurs often until a certain complicated piece of psychical work directed against it has been completed by the subject. The effect of *B* is not absurd, is comprehensible to the subject and can even be fought against by him" (406). It is thus the repression of memories that creates a hole in the network that is covered up by a substitute memory. Lacan is therefore correct in saying that the unconscious is structured like a language because Freud can only describe the workings of the primary process by utilizing the poetic forms of substitution (metaphor) and association (metonymy).[9] Furthermore, by equating memories with neurons and symbols, Freud anticipates here contemporary computer science, neuroscience, and structural linguistics.[10]

What then can make our emotions overwhelming and incomprehensible is that these subjective reactions are appropriate to memories that are not accessible to consciousness. Freud understands this structure by turning to a system of symbolic logic: "*B* stands in a particular relation to *A*. For there has been an event which consisted of *B* +*A*. *A* was a subsidiary circumstance, while *B* was well calculated to produce a lasting effect. The production of this event in memory now occurs as though *A* had taken *B's* place. *A* has become a substitute, a 'symbol', for B. Hence the incongruity; for *A* is accompanied by consequences which it does not seem to deserve, which are not appropriate to it" (406–407). As Lacan stresses, this process of substitution is called metaphor in poetry and linguistics, and we see here how our unconscious minds are natural poets because one memory substitutes for another memory in an automatic fashion.[11] This notion of the poetic mind then leads to the practice of free association because psychoanalysis works by retracing the network of memories in our mind to discover the repressed links and correct the displacement of emotion.

To further clarify the difference between the normal use of language and the hysterical discourse, Freud gives the following examples: "Symbols are formed in this way normally as well. A soldier will sacrifice himself for a piece of coloured cloth on a pole, because it has become the symbol of his native country; and no one considers this neurotic. But a hysterical symbol behaves differently. The knight who fights for a lady's glove *knows*, in the first place, that the glove owes its importance to the lady; and, secondly, his worship of the glove does not in the least prevent him from thinking of the lady and serving her in other ways. But the hysteric who is reduced to tears by *A* is unaware that this is because of the association *A-B*, and *B* itself plays no part whatever in his mental life. In this case the symbol has taken the place of the thing completely" (407).

This description of how language works in society is a great example of Lacan's notion that a signifier represents a subject for another signifier.[12] In the first case, the flag is a signifier that represents the nation for the soldier just as the glove represents the lady for the lover. Language thus works by connecting two different things through a repeated association. However, in the case of the unconscious, the symbol (flag, glove) takes the place of the thing it is supposed to represent (nation, lady).[13]

I am going over this model of mental functioning in detail because it will help me to later explain how emotions, fantasies, and unconscious desires function in everyday life, and what we will discover is that most people, even most psychoanalysts, understand little about the unconscious because they do not understand how the primary processes work. As we have seen, the unconscious is not some mythical or mystical entity; rather, it is based on a fairly logical system of symbolic connections, and this symbolic network is what allows free association to function so that we can take a scientific approach to our own thinking, emotions, and memories.

REPRESSION IN THE NETWORK

To help account for how the connections between our thoughts and memories become distorted, Freud introduces his theory of repression: "We can sum the matter up by saying that A is compulsive and B repressed (at least from consciousness). Analysis has revealed the surprising fact that for every compulsion there is a corresponding repression, that for every excessive irruption into consciousness there is a corresponding amnesia" (407). The great insight that Freud reveals here is that the displaced intensity of an emotion attached to a particular memory or thought is derived from the repression of an associated event. Freud adds that this process is initiated by an encounter with sexuality because sexual excitements conflict with the pleasure principle's goals of reducing tension and stimulation: "Repression is exclusively brought to bear on ideas that, firstly, arouse a distressing affect (unpleasure) in the ego, and that, secondly, relate to sexual life" (408). Here we find support for Lacan's claim that the reality of the unconscious is sexual: since the pleasure principle tries to escape stimulation, intense internal sexual feelings and experiences have to be repressed.[14]

The two main concerns of psychoanalysis, sexuality and the unconscious, are thus united in this theory of repression: "Experience shows, however, that the most distressing memories, which must necessarily arouse the greatest unpleasure (memories of remorse over bad actions), cannot be repressed and replaced by symbols. The existence of a second necessary precondition of pathological defence-sexuality-suggests that the explanation must be looked for elsewhere" (409). Freud claims here that memories of sexual feelings and encounters are repressed and substituted with symbols so that feelings of guilt and shame are not transformed into symbolic substitutes. In fact, Freud differentiates between hysterical emotions and obsessional ideas by arguing that in the case of obsessive-compulsive disorders, intense ideas occur without a substitute symbolization: "But we shall find when we come to analyse (for instance) obsessional neurosis that there repression occurs *without* symbolization, and, indeed, that repression and substitution are there separated in time" (410). The idea here is that in the case of obsessional neurosis, one first represses a memory, and then one later becomes aware of one's guilt. A key then to understanding obsessional neurosis is this temporal separation of repression from the substitute symptom.

A CASE OF HYSTERIA

To further explain how repression, sexuality, symptoms, and primary processes are related, Freud turns to case of a girl who developed the irrational fear of entering into stores by herself: "Emma is at the present time under a compulsion not to go into shops *alone*. She explained this by a memory dating from the age of twelve (shortly before her puberty). She went into a shop to buy something, saw the two shop-assistants (one of whom she remembers) laughing together, and rushed out in some kind *of fright*. In this connection it was possible to elicit the idea that the two men had been laughing at her clothes and that one of them had attracted her sexually" (410). At first, Freud is able to tie Emma's phobia to the bad encounter she had at a shop when a man who attracted her sexually laughed at her. However, things become much more complicated when Emma relates another earlier memory: "Further investigation brought to light a second memory, which she denies having had in mind at the moment of Scene I. Nor is there any evidence to support its presence there. On two occasions, when she was a child of eight, she had gone into a shop to buy some sweets and the shopkeeper had grabbed at her genitals through her clothes. In spite of the first experience she had gone to the shop a second time, after which she had stopped away. Afterwards she reproached herself for having gone the second time, as

though she had wanted to provoke the assault. And in fact a 'bad conscience' by which she was oppressed could be traced back to this experience" (411). In relating the first scene to the second earlier scene, Freud
is able to locate the missing memory that explains the current phobia.
Not only was Emma sexually assaulted as a girl, but she returned to the
same store at a later date, which made her feel guilty for her actions.
An important aspect to this story is that Emma is both attracted and
repulsed by her initial sexual encounter.

The complicated derivation of this hysterical symptom not only
reveals how the primary processes function in the unconscious, but
Freud also uses this example to introduce his important theory of sexual stages: "We can now understand Scene I (with the shop-assistants)
if we take it in conjunction with Scene II (with the shopkeeper). All we
need is an associative link between them. She herself remarked that a link
of this kind was provided by the *laughter*. The shop-assistants' laughter
had reminded her of the grin with which the shopkeeper had accompanied his assault. The whole process can now be reconstructed thus.
The two shop-assistants *laughed* in the shop, and this laughter (unconsciously) aroused the memory of the shopkeeper. The second situation
had the further point of similarity with the first that she was once again
in a shop alone. The shopkeeper's grabbing through her clothes was
remembered; but since then she had reached puberty. The recollection
aroused (what the event when it occurred could certainly not have done)
a sexual release, which turned into anxiety. In her anxiety she was afraid
the shop-assistants might repeat the assault, and ran away" (411). The
first thing to point out in this example is the way that the repetition of
laughter in two different events serves to connect together the different
memories. Moreover, Freud implies that at first, Emma was too young
to have sexual knowledge, so it was only after the fact when part of the
event was repeated that she was able to re-interpret the first event as
being traumatic. In other words, it was not the original sexual encounter that upset her; rather, her anxiety was generated when she entered
puberty and was able to understand the first event as being sexual in
nature. Freud will later explain this structure when he differentiates
between the three periods of sexuality: infantile, latency, and puberty.[15]
This theory is dialectical in nature because it is based on the idea that our
first experiences occur without knowledge and then those experiences
are either forgotten or negated, but they are later re-interpreted after the
fact when new knowledge is gained.[16]

One reason, then, why sexuality is tied to the unconscious is that early sexual experiences are separated from their meaning, and these events are only understood after the fact. In this structure, the latency period serves as a natural break in sexual activity, which serves as a form of repression separating an original event from its later understanding. Here we find the general structure of a symptom: an original fixation is repressed, and then it returns through a symbolic substitution in the form of a symptom, but in the case of hysteria, the new knowledge that re-interprets the original event is also repressed and replaced by isolated aspects of memory: "Although it is unusual in mental life for a memory to arouse an affect which the actual experience has not produced, this is nevertheless what quite ordinarily happens in the case of sexual ideas, precisely because the retardation of puberty is a general characteristic of the organization. Every adolescent carries memory-traces which can only be understood after his own sexual feelings have appeared; every adolescent, accordingly, must carry within him the germ of hysteria" (413). In this generalized theory of hysteria, we see how everyone is prone to the repression and return of sexual desires within the structure of the unconscious.

AFFECT VS. THOUGHT

Freud's next move is to argue that intense emotions block our ability to think and reflect in a rational way, and thus they can undermine the realty principle and our efforts to judge things in an impartial manner: "We know from everyday experiences that the generation of affect inhibits the normal course of thought, and that it does so in various ways. In the first place, many trains of thought may be forgotten which would otherwise be taken into account-as occurs, that is, in dreams. For instance, *it* has happened to me that in the agitation caused by a great anxiety I have forgotten to make use of the telephone, which had been introduced into my house a short time before. The recently established path succumbed to the state of affect. The facilitation-that is to say, what was old-established- won the day. Such forgetting involves the *loss* of the power of selection, of efficiency and of logic, just as happens in dreams" (414). Freud posits here hat anxiety can cause us to forget what we know and to think without logic, and therefore, the unconscious primary processes can be activated whenever we are feeling intense emotions. It is vital to highlight here the way that anxiety plays a key role in triggering unconscious primary processes that block reality testing.

On one level, Freud is repeating the old philosophical opposition of reason and emotion, but he adds a new twist by showing how emotions trigger unconscious thinking: "'Reflection' is an activity of the ego which demands time, and it becomes impossible when the affective level involves large quantities. Hence it is that where there is affect there is hastiness and a choice of methods similar to that made in the primary process" (415). Since we all experience feelings of haste and anxiety, Freud is no longer talking about neurotic distortions; rather, Freud is showing how the unconscious primary processes affect us on a daily basis. Just the mere fact of being in a hurry can make us regress in our thinking to the distorted logic of the unconscious. However, Freud also points to one of the solutions to this problem by indicating that eliminating haste and slowing down our thinking can help us to avoid primary processes.

According to the *Project*, our main defense against the primary processes and the generation of affect is the ego's use of mental attention: "Thus it is the business of the ego to permit no release of affect, since this would at the same time permit a primary process. Its best instrument for this purpose is the mechanism of attention. If a cathexis which releases unpleasure were able to escape attention, the ego's intervention would come too late. And this is precisely what happens in the case of the hysterical *proton pseudos* [first lie]. Attention is focused on perceptions, which are the normal occasions for the release of unpleasure. But here it is not a perception but a memory-trace which unexpectedly releases unpleasure, and the ego discovers this too late. It has permitted a primary process, because it did not expect one" (415–416). Freud wants to say that we can avoid the primary processes if we pay attention and anticipate events that generate anxiety, but what happens in hysteria is that events occur before they are anticipated. The problem with this explanation is that Freud will later discover that what in part defines obsessional neurosis is precisely this attempt to anticipate anxiety-provoking situations through the act of obsessive attention and thinking.[17] One reason, then, why obsessionals have a hard time sleeping is that they try to anticipate every bad thing that could happen to them.

As we shall see in the next chapter, Freud continues his *Project* by outlining what will later become his theory of transference. His basic idea is that when we are unable to escape reality through the primary processes, we are forced to turn to the help of others to make our displeasure go away. We shall see how this demand for the Other to provide love, attention, and knowledge helps to explain why people submit to authority and believe in imaginary gods. However, before we move to the theme of transference, I want to stress that Freud's notion of the primary process reveals that we are able to escape reality and achieve the goals of the pleasure principle through the pure mechanism of unconscious thought, which satisfies our wishes but sacrifices the control we have over our own thinking and life.

On a social basis, the primary processes in the unconscious help us to understand how people can submit to authoritarian leaders and imaginary ideologies. Not only do we suspend our reality testing when we subject ourselves to a powerful leader, but we also engage in paranoid thinking as we see the world from a total ideological perspective. One reason, therefore, why people refuse to accept the reality of the world and their own lives is that they are prone to use their unconscious to satisfy their desires on a purely mental level. Although in the last chapter, I pointed to the destructive effects of drugs and media pleasure, what I highlighted in this chapter is that we do not even have to use an external object to escape from reality. It is as if we have a drug dealer and a movie theater in our own minds.

NOTES

1. Freud, *Project*, 380.
2. Lacan calls this wishes desires, and stresses how desire is always caused by a lack of satisfaction.
3. Descartes, René. *Discourse on Method and the Meditations.* Penguin Books, 1968.
4. Lacan, *Four*, 30–32.
5. A great limitation of Lacan's work is that he intends to downplay the role of the ego in reality testing because he sees the ego as primarily a defensive and imaginary agency.
6. Freud, *Totem*, 120.
7. Silber, Austin. "Secondary revision, secondary elaboration and ego synthesis." *International Journal of Psycho-Analysis* 54 (1973): 161–168.
8. Lacan, *Four*, 237.
9. Lacan, Jacques. "The seminar of Jacques Lacan: Book V: The formations of the unconscious: 1957–1958." (2011).
10. Gleick, James. "The information: A history, a theory, a flood (Gleick, J.; 2011) [Book Review]." *IEEE Transactions on Information Theory* 57.9 (2011): 6332–6333.

11. Lacan, Jacques. "The function and field of speech and language in psychoanalysis." *Écrits: A Selection* (1977): 30–113.
12. See chapter one of Lacan, Jacques. *The Other Side of Psychoanalysis.* W. W. Norton, 2007.
13. Following Lacan's logic in *The Other Side of Psychoanalysis*, we can say that the discourse of the hysteric displaces the discourse of the master by replacing the primary signifier (S1) with the related signified (S2).
14. Lacan, *Four*, 254.
15. Freud, Sigmund. *Three Essays on the Theory of Sexuality: The 1905 Edition.* Verso Books, 2017.
16. Many of Freud's theories are Hegelian in structure without any evidence that Freud was influenced by Hegel.
17. Freud, Sigmund. "Notes upon a case of obsessional neurosis." *The Standard Edition of the Complete Psychological Works of Sigmund Freud, Volume X (1909): Two Case Histories ('Little Hans' and the 'Rat Man').* 1955. 151–318.

CHAPTER 5

Transference and Narcissism

Abstract This chapter discusses how Freud's theory of transference and narcissism relate to the way that we make a call to others to fix reality and help us satisfy the pleasure principle. Not only do we turn to others to satisfy our desires, but we want our others to verify our sense of being good and right. Moreover, this structure of obsessional narcissism helps to explain the limitations of contemporary liberalism and the failure of many forms of analysis and therapy.

Keywords Freud · Transference · Narcissism · Obsessional · Liberalism

Throughout this book, I have focused my attention on interpreting Freud's *Project for a Scientific Psychology* because I believe that this text provides a structure for linking together in a logical order all of Freud's major ideas. On the most basic level, Freud articulates how we are driven to avoid tension through the activation of the pleasure principle, and the first way that we achieve this goal is through the primary processes in the unconscious, which use repression, substitution, displacement, and hallucination to imagine the satisfaction of our desires. Since the pleasure principle is opposed to the reality principle, the unconscious conflicts with our ability to test reality and apply reason and logic in an impartial way, and this lack of reason undermines global progress and personal well-being. In this chapter, I reveal Freud's next theory, which he will later call transference.

© The Author(s) 2019
R. Samuels, *Freud for the Twenty-First Century*,
https://doi.org/10.1007/978-3-030-24382-1_5

43

TRANSFERENCE

The most common understanding of transference is the notion that when people go into psychoanalysis, they end up falling in love with their analyst. While I would not dispute that this does happen, it is only a particular example of a more subtle dynamic that occurs in everyday life, which involves the way we turn to other people in order to realize the goal of the pleasure principle. In the *Project*, Freud introduces this fundamental human relationship in the following manner: "Here a removal of the stimulus can only be effected by an intervention which will temporarily stop the release of quantity in the interior of the body, and an intervention of this kind requires an alteration in the external world (e.g., the supply of nourishment or the proximity of the sexual object), and this, as a 'specific action', can only be brought about in particular ways. At early stages the human organism is incapable of achieving this specific action. It is brought about by extraneous help, when the attention of an experienced person has been drawn to the child's condition by a discharge taking place along the path of internal change [e.g., by the child's screaming]. This path of discharge thus acquires an extremely important secondary function- viz., of bringing about an understanding with other people; and the original helplessness of human beings is thus the primal source of all moral motives" (379). There is a lot to unpack in this passage because it defines Freud's fundamental theory of how we become social beings. While the infant is first able to satisfy his or her desires by hallucinating the fulfillment of wishes, when this unconscious activity does not achieve its goal of reducing tension and enacting the pleasure principle, the next step is for the helpless child to cry for the help of another person who can change reality and satisfy the desire. Freud adds that this initial relationship between the helpless child and the helping other determines morality and social communication.

Social language and morality are therefore derived in an act of transference because the helpless subject uses an expressed sign to get the help of another person. As Lacan stresses, the initial demand that we make to our caregivers is a demand for unconditional love, recognition, and understanding, but because this demand is produced within language, our natural needs become distorted through symbolic representations.[1] For instance, when a child asks for food, the child also desires love and recognition, but the language of the demand is only directed towards a particular object. Moreover, the original need is turned into a social request that replaces our natural instincts with human drives. When Freud argues that the crying for food and attention of the helpless baby introduces morality and communication into the human subject, he points to this fundamental relationship between human beings: "This total event then constitutes an 'experience of satisfaction', which has the most momentous consequences in the functional development of the individual. For three things occur in his system: (I) A lasting discharge is effected, so that the urgency which had generated unpleasure ... is brought to an end. (2) A cathexis corresponding to the perception of an object occurs in one or more neurones of the pallium. (3) At other points of the pallium a report is received of the discharge brought about by the release of the reflex movement which followed the specific action. A facilitation is then established between these cathexes [(2) and (3)] and the nuclear neurones [which were being cathected from endogenous sources during the state of urgency]" (374). This is a complicated way of saying that when the other helps the child, the pleasure principle is achieved, and the child makes a mental connection between the helping other and the feeling of pleasure. We find here the origin of love in the form of care and understanding.

Until the child cries for the help of the parent, the pleasure principle is achieved through the pure mental process of hallucinating the satisfaction of desire, but when this process fails to achieve its goal, one is forced to make a call for help, which can only be successful if the other person understands what is being demanded. Communication and mutual understanding have to function in order for the other person to comply with the demand of the subject. Here we enter into the social world of human beings, which requires many different psychological and linguistic elements: "Let us suppose that the object presented by the perception is similar to the [percipient] subject himself-that is to say, a fellow human-being. The theoretical interest taken in it is then further explained by the fact that an object *of a similar kind* was the subject's first satisfying object (and also his first hostile object) as well as his sole assisting force. For this reason it is on his fellow-creatures that a human being first learns to cognize" (393). Freud's argument is therefore that our original relationship with our caregivers determines how we will think and act in the future. He also adds that this first helping other is experienced in an ambivalent way as being both a hostile and assisting object. Lacan will explain this ambivalence in his theory of the mirror stage, where he shows how we identify with other people in order to gain a sense of self, but these other people are also our rivals.[2]

Since we first learn about ourselves by looking at others and mirroring their responses, the initial demand for love, recognition, and understanding has to be understood in a dual relationship that is prone to competition, envy, and jealousy. For if we idealize the other as the one who can fix our problems, then we also may experience this dependency through feelings of resentment.[3] Due to the fact that our initial relation to others is through a mirroring experience, we often project our aggression onto other people, and we experience their feelings as coming from our own selves. Lacan calls this mental transitivism, which Freud understands as a basic form of empathy and communicative understanding[4]: "The perceptual complexes arising from this fellow-creature will in part be new and non- comparable-for instance, its features (in the visual sphere); but other visual perceptions (for instance, the movements of its hands) will coincide in the subject with his own memory of quite similar visual impressions of his own body-a memory with which will be associated memories of movements experienced by himself. The same will be the case with other perceptions of the object; thus, for instance, if the object screams, a memory of the subject's own screaming will be aroused and will consequently revive his own experiences of pain. Thus the complex of a fellow-creature falls into two portions. One of these gives the impression of being a constant structure and remains as a coherent 'thing'; while the other can be *understood* by the activity of memory-that is, can be traced back to information about the subject's own body" (393–394). Just as Lacan argues that we first gain a sense of our body and self as being unified and coherent by seeing an image in a mirror, Freud shows how we gain information about our own body by seeing the shared characteristics of similar bodies. Freud adds that when the other person cries, we can also feel their pain by remembering how we felt when we cried.

Freud thus places the initial demand to the other within a context of mirroring relationships, which he will later define as narcissism.[5] By combining the cry to the other for help and the discovery of the self through mirroring, Freud presents transference as both the formation of the ego and the submission to the other. To clarify this structure, Lacan describes a scene where a parent holds a child up in front of the mirror, and the child first looks at his image and then looks back at the parent who is also looking at the image in the mirror. Using Freud's later terminology, Lacan argues that the ideal ego is being recognized by the ego-ideal, and here we find the foundation of the idealizing transference.[6] The child then will start to see himself from the perspective of the other, as the good self is recognized by the idealized other.

Transference, then, does not just happen in analytic treatment; rather, the idealizing transference explains obsessional narcissism and the need to have our idealized self verified by other people. For instance, on Facebook, people post pictures of themselves doing great things, and they want other people to see and "like" their self-presentations. In the case of obsessional neurosis, Freud discovered that his patients wanted their analyst to recognize their goodness, and so they did not want to talk about anything that made them look bad.[7]

Analysis can only make progress if the analyst finds a way to subvert the idealization and narcissistic transference because without this move, the patient will only try to impress the analyst by showing off his good side and hiding his bad side. In fact, the ego ideal functions to repress the super-ego into the unconscious so that the subject does not have to confront his guilt and shame. We find an example of this structure in what we can call liberal narcissism: people want to see themselves being good by showing off to others their good acts and intentions, but Lacan argues that these conspicuous displays of altruism usually hide an under-lying aggression.[8]

LIBERAL NARCISSISM

Psychoanalysis teaches us the hard lesson that not only do people become dependent on others because they want them to solve all of their problems, but the pleasure principle is achieved when we get others to recognize our own good intentions. We thus idealize others, and then we ask these idealized others to verify our goodness, and at first, there seems nothing wrong with this structure, but what we discover in analysis is that narcissistic love and transference rely on reducing other people to simply responding positively to our unconditional demands for love, understanding, and recognition.

In the case of politics, we can see the limitations of liberal narcissism in instances where policies fail, but they are never corrected because that would mean admitting a mistake and recognizing one's own bad actions. If politicians only do and say things to make others like them and recognize them as being good, then these politicians will never confront their own mistakes or admit the limits of their own knowledge and abilities. Since the reality principle entails that we confront conflicts and upsetting realities, liberal narcissism often serves as a resistance to the reality principle and the impartial judgment of empirical evidence.

Liberal narcissism can also be seen through the emphasis on education as the solution to all of our economic and social problems.[9] The current dominant liberal ideology is meritocracy, which argues that by doing well in education, one can make sure that one will have a good life. This system is founded on the idea that one's good self has to be recognized by the ideal other in the form of grades, degrees, and the constant assessment of talent and ability. In the meritocratic structure, self-worth is defined by educational attainment, and thus one becomes dependent on the judgment of others.

A great example of meritocracy can be seen in the film *The Wizard of Oz*. When Dorothy and her friends finally meet the wizard and ask for him to satisfy their demands for knowledge, courage, and love, the wizard gives the scarecrow a diploma, and suddenly this man who thought he was born without a brain is able to say a complicated mathematical formula. The idea appears to be that we need external signs of recognition to prove to others and our own self our inner value and worth. Education here is reduced to the conferring of signs of value by the ideal other. The problem is that education should be about the discovery of the truth about our selves and the world around us through the scientific use of the reality principle, but what has happened is that science has been replaced by narcissistic transference.

RETURN TO REALITY

Freud argues in the *Project* that the main way to overcome the pleasure principle and submit to the reality principle is to move beyond the primary processes and transference by first distinguishing between memories and perceptions: "Accordingly, *it is the inhibition brought about by the ego that makes possible a criterion for distinguishing between a perception and a memory*" (388). Since we are prone to confuse our memories of pleasure with our perceptions of the external world, it is necessary for the ego to inhibit this enactment of the pleasure principle. The first way this separation occurs for Freud is when one seeks out a desired object, but one realizes that this object is only an image and is not present in reality: "The first of these arises if, while it is in a wishful state, it freshly cathects the memory of the object and then sets the process of discharge in motion, where there can be no satisfaction because the object is not present *really* but only as an imaginary idea" (386). In other words, the subject first has to imagine an object of satisfaction, and then the subject has to accept that the object is not there in reality. Here we encounter Lacan's theory of the object *a* as a part of the real that resists being included into the imaginary world of images and satisfaction.[10] The reality principle thus requires a disinvestment in imaginary pleasure and the unconscious fulfillment of wishes.

Freud holds out the hope that the self can be educated, and that the reality principle can be attained as a new, but inhibited version of the pleasure principle: "The education and development of this original ego take place in states in which there is a repetition of the craving, in states of *expectation*. The ego learns first that it must not cathect the motor images (with consequent discharge), until certain conditions have been fulfilled on the perceptual side. It learns further that it must not cathect the wishful idea beyond a certain degree, because, if it does, it will deceive itself in a hallucinatory manner. If, however, it respects these two restrictions and turns its attention to the new perceptions, it has a prospect of attaining the desired satisfaction" (426–427). While the reality principle is in opposition to the pleasure principle, Freud affirms that even the reality principle achieves the aims of pleasure, and yet, he also posits that we can only learn by accepting displeasure: "Unpleasure remains the sole means of education" (428). From this perspective, discontent in civilization and education is necessary because one can only learn by giving up the imaginary object of our desire as we confront the lack of the object in the real.

Unfortunately, in our current educational environment, many people want to go against the necessary discomfort of the reality principle by creating safe spaces as places where people do not have to encounter upsetting ideas or different perspectives. On one level, the use of safe spaces and trigger warnings represent a desire to avoid conflict and tension caused by the encounter with hate speech. However, on another level, these educational structures serve to reinforce obsessional narcissism as people are able to retreat to a world where their good self is affirmed by a supportive Other. What then bothers many people about political correctness is that it seems to be forced and fake in its efforts to police verbal aggression. From a psychoanalytic perspective, the real problem is that political correctness can silence teachers and students and prevent them from dealing with the realities of the world.[11]

THE LANGUAGE PROBLEM

Freud's model is rendered complex by his realization that the only way we can approach the real is if we use speech, but this use of the symbolic must be detached from transference and the primary processes: "*Thus, thought which is accompanied by the cathexis of indications of thought-reality or of indications of speech is the highest and most secure form of cognitive thought-process*" (431). The paradox here is that thought and speech can mislead us, but in the end, all we have is language to approach reality. As Lacan argues, the word may be the death of the thing, but it is only through the word that the absence of the object can be recognized.[12]

Since speech in the form of free association is the only medium of psychoanalysis, it is necessary to use language to approach reality, and this requires differentiating between what Freud calls practical and theoretical thought: "It is interesting to observe how *practical* thought lets itself be directed by the biological rule of defence. In *theoretical* (cognitive and critical) thought, the rule is no longer observed. This is intelligible; for in purposive thinking it is a question of finding *some* path and those paths to which unpleasure attaches can be excluded, whereas in theoretical thinking *every* path has to be investigated" (440). This idea of following every path of thought and not ignoring the ones that generate displeasure represents Freud's application of science to everyday life.

As we shall see in the next chapter, this effort of implementing the reality principle to pursue personal well-being and global progress is blocked by misunderstandings concerning how psychoanalysis, democratic law, and science achieve their goals. When people combine the pleasure principle, unconscious primary processes, and transference together, they submit to destructive ideologies countering our global progress and our pursuit of truth.

NOTES

1. Lacan, *Four*, 154–156.
2. Lacan, Jacques. "The mirror stage as formative of the function of the I as revealed in psychoanalytic experience (1949)." *Reading French Psychoanalysis*. Routledge, 2014. 119–126.
3. Lacan, Jacques. "Aggressivity in psychoanalysis." *Écrits: A Selection* (1977): 8–29.
4. Lacaan, *Mirror*, 5.

5. Freud, Sigmund. *On Narcissism: An Introduction*. Read Books Ltd., 2014.
6. Lacan, *Four*, 257.
7. Freud, Sigmund. "Notes upon a case of obsessional neurosis." *The Standard Edition of the Complete Psychological Works of Sigmund Freud, Volume X (1909): Two Case Histories ('Little Hans' and the 'Rat Man')*. 1955. 151–318.
8. Lacan, Jacques. "Aggressivity in psychoanalysis." *Écrits: A Selection* (1977): 8–29.
9. Samuels, Robert. *Educating Inequality: Beyond the Political Myths of Higher Education and the Job Market*. Routledge, 2017.
10. Lacan, *Four*, 77.
11. Fairclough, Norman. "'Political correctness': The politics of culture and language." *Discourse & Society* 14.1 (2003): 17–28.
12. Lacan, Jacques. "The subversion of the subject and the dialectic of desire in the Freudian unconscious." *Hegel and Contemporary Continental Philosophy* 19.6 (1960): 205–235.

CHAPTER 6

The Resistances to Psychoanalysis
and Global Progress

Abstract This chapter examines some of the many ways that people misunderstand psychoanalysis and global progress. In reviewing the distorted interpretations of the pleasure principle, the reality principle, the primary processes, and transference, I reveal how psychoanalysis has been repressed from within psychoanalysis itself. I also connect this repression to the ways people deny the evidence concerning our global progress.

Keywords Global progress · Ideology · Psychoanalysis · Reality principle

Before I read Steven Pinker's *Enlightenment Now*, I had no idea about how much progress we have made globally in terms of life expectancy, human rights, individual freedom, and economic mobility. Like most people, I assumed that the state of the world was getting worse, and that we were now entering a dark period full of prejudice, inequality, and authoritarian government. It is therefore important to ask how could I and so many other people be so wrong?

One cause for this ignorance is of course the media, which attracts and maintains our attention by presenting us with threatening information.[1] However, various modes of media only work if we desire to see what they are showing. It is therefore incorrect to simply blame the media since we are driven to consume it. Perhaps we are programmed by natural selection to monitor our environment for threatening stimuli;

© The Author(s) 2019
R. Samuels, *Freud for the Twenty-First Century*,
https://doi.org/10.1007/978-3-030-24382-1_6

however, psychoanalysis tells us that the pleasure principle drives us to avoid all displeasure and conflict, so it is hard to see why we would be fixated on viewing negative information.

This focus on the negative and the threatening can be in part explained by the primary processes and the ways the unconscious turns every representation into a source of pleasure. Moreover, if one of the goals of the pleasure principle is to deny any sense of guilt, shame, or responsibility, then the media offer us a perfect opportunity to see pain and suffering at a distance without any direct involvement. As we sit safely in our living rooms and watch the negative representations of the world on the television set, we are reduced to being a pure, uninvolved spectator. Interestingly, when Freud talks about fantasies of abuse in his text, "A Child is Being Beaten," he argues that the first level of the fantasy involves the patient as a detached observer watching the suffering of several boys.[2] From this perspective, we can see how popular culture caters to our voyeuristic and sadistic desires to witness the suffering of others. The difficult conclusion that we can draw from this theory of cultural fantasy is that not only do people enjoy the suffering of others, but this internalization of negative images creates a negative view about the world around us.[3]

Of course it is not only the media that represents negative aspects of the world; politicians often gain power by telling people that the world is falling apart, and they are the solution. In this form of transference, the negative portrayal of the world scares people into turning to a powerful savior, and it is this type of relationship that Erich Fromm describes in his *Escape from Freedom.*[4] Clearly in the return to authoritarian government and religious fundamentalism in different parts of the world, we are witnessing a resistance to global progress based on a desire to re-establish a lost authority of order and control. In this mode of transference, people give up their own freedom and responsibility and turn to a powerful Other to fix all of the world's problems.

TRUMP AND TRANSFERENCE

Freud's theory of transference can help us to understand why people support someone like Donald Trump. As Trump himself said during his campaign, he could shoot someone in the middle of the street, and he would not lose any supporters. What Trump exposed in this statement was the idea that his followers had given up all reality testing, and they had surrendered their own morality and will to their all-powerful leader. In a previous book, I argued that Trump can be seen as representing a type of wild psychoanalysis because he often says all of the things you are not supposed to say in public.[5] In fact, what attracts many of his followers is that he appears to be free of the oppressive liberal super-ego, and therefore he represents a truth-teller who is real and authentic and is not afraid to offend other people. While the opposition sees him as the most deceitful president ever, his followers experience him as the most truthful.

In the relationship of transference between him and his followers, Trump represents the idealized primitive father who has free access to total enjoyment. Instead of people resenting this display of wealth and excess, his supporters identify with it. For instance, after it was revealed that he said that when you are rich and famous, you can grab any woman anywhere you want, this display of obscene pleasure and power was allowed by his followers. Since they would also like to be able to do and say whatever they want, they find a sense of freedom and enjoyment by identifying with the powerful master. In fact, Freud argues that we love others who appear to have access to an unconstrained narcissism.

While many liberals believe that empathy and identification are the key to human rights and global justice, we see in the relationship between Trump and his followers the negative and destructive side of empathy and identification.[6] After all, his followers would let him get away with murder and sexual assault because they identify with his power and feel what he feels. As Paul Bloom points out in his book, *Against Empathy*, we often only identify with and feel empathy for people we know or others who look like us or come from the same social and ethnic group. Moreover, empathy can be very patronizing and short-term, and it often has a hard time dealing with large numbers of people. As Stalin argued, a single death is a tragedy, but a thousand deaths are a statistic. It is therefore hard to see how empathy can be the cause of global justice, if global human rights requires us to support billions of people we will never know and who do not come from the same ethnic or racial group.

Empathy is also a contentious issue in the field of psychoanalysis. Many analysts and therapists have moved away from free association and the neutrality of the analyst because they believe that it is important to understand and empathize with their patients.[7] These therapists and theorists do not understand that psychoanalysis only works if the analyst refuses to be a source of recognition, knowledge, and love for the patient. It is by not satisfying the demand for transference that the patients are able to discover the source of their fundamental desires. Moreover, if the reality principle requires encountering the loss of the object of satisfaction, then analysts have to eventually embody this loss. Instead, many analysts and therapists feed the transference and allow for the activation of the primary processes in the unconscious. One reason for this avoidance of analytic neutrality is that it feels good to be the idealized Other who knows and understands.

As Lacan insisted throughout his work, Freud's basic ideas and practices have been repressed by analysts because they do not understand the theories, and they would rather be seen as the source of idealization for their patients. In this structure, the analyst wants to be the savior of the patient, but much of Freud's work was dedicated to freeing people from their dependency on others in order for them to live a free and truthful life.

Therapists also undermine analysis because they replace free association with face-to-face conversation. These pseudo-analysts simply refuse to understand why it is important to let the patients say whatever comes to their minds. They also do not see why it is necessary to remove the look of the analyst, so that one can speak without self-censoring. When analysts fail to be neutral, and they do not enable free association, they end up activating the combination of the pleasure principle, the unconscious primary process, and the narcissistic transference as they avoid the reality principle. It is often the therapists' own obsessional desires to understand everything and to be desired and loved by others that pushes them to reject the fundamental practices of psychoanalysis.

Since it is now in vogue to argue that it is impossible to be neutral, therapists reject the very principle of analytic neutrality. Many therapists feel that it is simply too cold and impersonal to listen to someone without engaging in a conversation, and so they have embraced an inter-subjective model of therapy, which simply relies on using the normal modes of communication. One reason why they may not accept the fundamental rules of analysis is that they do not believe that truth will eventually be discovered because they do not believe in Freud's fundamental insight that memories cannot be erased. Furthermore, the narcissism of the therapist is enhanced when their patients see them as good people with good intentions trying to help others. Since they think that empathy is the main tool for the cure, they feel quite comfortable projecting their own feelings and ideas onto their patents. What they do not want to accept is the idea that on a fundamental level, perfect communication is impossible because we never really know what another person is thinking or feeling.

Ultimately, it is the failure to understand the meaning of the reality principle, the pleasure principle, unconscious primary processes, and transference that prevents analysts and therapist from helping their patients discover the reality of their own lives. In short, therapists often do not help people to apply the scientific method to their own memories, thoughts, and feelings. A major reason for this repression of psychoanalysis from within psychoanalysis is that it is very difficult to talk and think about the unconscious. When we normally use language, we assume that we are in control of what we say and that we are aware of the meaning of our own words. However, with the primary processes in the unconscious, we do not have control of our representations. For instance, think of any dream, and you will realize that you did not intend to see what you saw. Moreover, the very idea of repression goes against our most basic self-understanding. After all, how can we hide things from ourselves; if there is anything we know, it is our own thoughts and feelings. Yet, psychoanalysis tells us that we are constantly lying to ourselves to make us feel good and to enact the dictates of the pleasure principle.

Freud's concept of secondary revision helps to explain why and how we cover over our own unconscious by retelling things from the perspective of intention and conscious awareness. In fact, a defining aspect of obsessional neurosis is the rewriting of history after the fact in order to escape feelings of guilt and shame. Since we want to believe that we are in control of our own minds, we have to retroactively rationalize our thoughts and behaviors. Freud first discovered this tendency when he was using hypnosis, and after he suggested someone to do something, they would later act as if it was their own choice. For example, you can hypnotize someone and tell them to walk like a chicken, and once you wake them from their trance, and you ask them what they were doing, they will instantly explain that they wanted to do a funny dance. This post-hypnotic rationalization points to the way that we constantly turn ideas and desires that come from others into our own intentions.

If psychoanalysis deals with thoughts that are unintentional, then it runs into the problem of people trying to explain away this lack of intention and control. Furthermore, from the perspective of many neuroscientists and evolutionary psychologists, we often make a quick non-conscious decision based on inherited mental programs lodged in the right part of our brains, and then afterwards, we create a rationalization using the left part of our brain.[8] The only problems with this theory, and much of neuroscience and evolutionary psychology, is that it relies on the notion that our unconscious is derived from inherited mental constructs internalized through natural selection.[9] This theory represses repression and ignores the way humans break with nature and evolution through language and culture. After all, a fundamental claim of psychoanalysis is that our basic needs are distorted and disrupted by society and culture, and so our natural impulses are transformed into drives.

As I discussed in the chapter on transference, when humans desire something, they often make a request to others, but this demand is not just for the asked for object; instead, people make a demand for unconditional love, recognition, and understanding. Furthermore, it is not only social dictates that prohibit our natural sexual and aggressive impulses, but our own pleasure principle limits and represses our desires. Since neuroscientists and evolutionary psychologists tend to dismiss the important roles language and culture play in transforming our impulses into desires, they are unable to understand the unconscious and the pleasure principle.

THE CULTURE OF CONFLICT

A related way that psychoanalysis becomes repressed is the belief that therapy should be about liberating our impulses and making us free of conflict.[10] The problem with this idea is that psychoanalysis is about discovering the truth of the self, and our selves are conflicted. As Freud insists in *Civilization and Its Discontents*, there is a fundamental, unresolvable conflict between society and the individual, and even though the pleasure principle would like to repress this conflict, there is no way to escape it, and so we must learn how to accept it, and work with it.

Since we cannot completely erase our own memories and thoughts, we cannot escape our sense of guilt and shame generated by the super-ego. This realization of unconscious conflict was at the heart of Shakespeare's work, and we see in the most famous speech in Western literature why we cannot escape our own conscience:

> To be, or not to be--that is the question:
> ... To die, to sleep--
> . . To sleep--perchance to dream: ay, there's the rub,

For in that sleep of death what dreams may come
.. To grunt and sweat under a weary life,
But that the dread of something after death,
The undiscovered country, from whose bourn
No traveller returns, puzzles the will,
... Thus conscience does make cowards of us all...
The fair Ophelia! ... Be all my sins remember'd.[11]

The first thing I want to highlight is that Hamlet is arguing that the main reason why he does not want to kill himself is that he is afraid of the judgment of his act that will be made in purgatory. This religious belief in purgatory is then transformed into a theory of the unconscious since Hamlet equates what happens after death with the dreams one has when one is asleep. From Hamlet's perspective, we cannot escape our conscience because it is lodged in our unconscious, and it is therefore the unconscious conscience that makes us ethical.

One lesson we can learn from Hamlet is that we cannot try to avoid our own guilt and shame because truth will eventually emerge. In fact, Hamlet ends by telling Ophelia that she will embody his remembered sins, and Shakespeare had the profound insight that truth will always come out in the end through the unconscious. This is why in *The Merchant of Venice*, we are told, "truth will come to light; murder cannot be hid long; a man's son may, but at the length truth will out." By saying that truth will out, Shakespeare reveals his anticipation of Freud's thought: they both believe that due to the impossibility of erasing memories, we cannot escape the truth, and this is what makes us ethical subjects. Lady Macbeth can never wash away the bloodstains, and we can never stop truth from escaping from our mouths during free association.

ZIZEK AND THE REPRESSION OF PSYCHOANALYSIS

A paradox of psychoanalysis is that it is hard to represent, but we cannot escape it because we cannot avoid the truth of our unconscious. A great example of this revelation and repression of analysis can be found in the work of Slavoj Zizek. Many people today first learn about psychoanalysis through Zizek's work, and so he has a great deal of influence on the current reception of this field. However, it will be my argument that while Zizek does use a lot of psychoanalytic terminology, he represses analysis by transforming psychoanalysis into an academic discourse. In fact, by seeing how he represents the theories of the pleasure principle, the reality principle, the unconscious, and transference, we can gain a better understanding of why psychoanalysis is so misunderstood.

Although Zizek spends a great deal of time writing and talking about enjoyment, he never appears to have understood Freud's basic insight that the pleasure principle is focused on avoiding tension and stimulation. For instance, in his translation of the French term "jouissance" into "enjoyment," Zizek eliminates the radical nature of pleasure in psychoanalysis.[12] Instead of seeing pleasure as a mostly defensive and repressive drive, Zizek tends to see it as a form of positive enjoyment. Moreover, as I have discussed in my chapter on the pleasure principle, Zizek never comes to terms with his own use of jokes and popular culture to entertain his audience. Since Freud believes that the audience is bribed with enjoyment so that they will not criticize the speaker, we can infer that Zizek unconsciously uses humor in part to block the criticism of his work. He thus is able to make sexist and racist jokes and avoid any personal responsibility because he is bent on bringing enjoyment to his audience. He gives them pleasure, and in turn, they implicitly agree to not criticize him or hold him responsible for what he says. It is therefore both on the level of performance and content that we see a major problem in his work.

By not understanding how the pleasure principle works, Zizek represses this concept as he combines high theory with "low" culture. For instance, his use of jokes is often combined with an attack on political correctness, which unintentionally replicates the Right-wing attack on the liberal super-ego. Although I do agree with many of his criticisms of excessive political correctness, he tends to ignore the fact that the basic idea behind this monitoring of speech is to not say hateful things about particular social groups. In a way, Zizek is intolerant of tolerance and tolerant of intolerance, and this performance of being free from social dictates makes him attractive to people who would also like to escape from the social censor.

Related to his use of jokes and popular culture is his constant repetition of the same material. One way of explaining this repetition compulsion is to affirm Lacan's idea that unconscious repetition concerns our attempt to use language to reach a reality that we can never fully attain.[13] It is my contention that since Zizek does not use the Freudian notion of the reality principle, he is stuck constantly trying to use his discourse to present a reality that always escapes him. In fact, he tends to argue that the Real is presented by the failures of the symbolic order, and so all we can do is repeat this failure in an obsessive way. There is simply no space in his work for the relation between the reality principle and science. One of the major reasons for Zizek's distortion of psychoanalysis is that he tends to try to use philosophy, politics, culture, and religion to understand the transference. Instead of relating free association to the neutrality of the analyst, he tends to use Hegel as his ideal dead Other who always already knows the meaning of everything. Hegel then is positioned to be Zizek's ideal Other who recognizes Zizek's ideal self.

Lacan was fond of saying that for the obsessional, the father is always dead because this symbolic Other can never talk back or criticize the subject.[14] In the performance of his work, Zizek's audience often stands in for the dead father because they are usually not provided with any opportunity to engage in a dialogue with him. Zizek is himself aware of this dynamic because he has commented on several occasions that he keeps speaking so that the other has no opportunity to intervene. In fact, he has compared this strategy to his own analysis where he said that he would plan out what he would say so that he could keep talking without interruption. Here we see how verbal and intellectual activity can act as an avoidance of the analytic process.

Perhaps the most telling way that Zizek represses psychoanalysis is through his own writing and speaking from a position of intentionality and conscious knowledge. As an example of the discourse of the university and secondary revision, Zizek reverses the unconscious by submitting all experience to a knowledge that is already there in the history of thought.[15] In his constant attempt to combine Hegel and Lacan, he seeks a mental mediation of conflicting discourses. While Hegel was able to combine religion and science by using the word Geist, which could mean both mind and spirit, Zizek uses his manipulation of language to resolve conflicts and thus achieve the goal of the pleasure principle. Through the process of secondary revision, the unconscious is repressed and the reality principle is avoided as real material conflicts are mediated in the realm of pure thought and language. Just as Marx was said to reverse Hegel by turning his idealism into materialism, Zizek seeks to reverse Marx's reversal.

One reason why I am focusing on all of these ways that psychoanalysis is being repressed is because one of my central claims is that we have never needed psychoanalysis more both on an individual and cultural level. On the one hand, we have to learn how to delay the pleasure principle and use the reality principle to discover the truth of our world, and on the other hand, we have to understand how drugs, media pleasure, political ideologies, and the submission to authoritarian leaders represent the biggest obstacles to continued global progress.

FROM THE PERSONAL TO THE GLOBAL

I have argued in this book that the many of the same things that make global progress possible are shared by the psychoanalytic process. In both cases, we need an impartial judge who examines evidence in an open and coherent way. Of course this effort to remain neutral and fair is an impossible ideal, and yet we strive to attain equality and justice. Moreover, just like science, democratic law is always a work in progress, and that is why we need social movements to protest when justice is unfair and certain groups are excluded from the system. What many liberals and conservatives fail to see is that part of our global progress has been derived from the efforts of minority-based social movements to expand universal justice and reverse the inherited premodern hierarchies based on prejudice and exploitation.[16] However, these same social movements can undermine global progress when they become fixated on their own grievances, and they stop pursuing equal treatment under the law.

To understand how Left-wing social movements can both help and undermine global progress, we can return to Freud's theory of fantasy and the primary processes in the unconscious. On one level, the fight for women's rights, civil rights, workers' rights, and gay rights has resulted in an expansion of global human rights.[17] Moreover, these groups have often gained attention and solidarity by pointing to a founding trauma or abuse. Yet, on another level, the identification around a victim identity can be highly destructive and counter-productive. Since the victim is always positioned to be innocent and pure, you cannot criticize the victim, and the vengeance by the victim is always justified.[18] Even by writing the previous sentence, I open myself up for being attacked for not protecting the victim. However, psychoanalysis has had a complex relationship with claims of victimization.

As many people know, Freud first believed that all of his female patients were actually sexually assaulted by their fathers, but he later began to discover that some of these women may have only fantasized about their abuse.[19] This controversial theory looks a lot like blaming the victim and denying the real suffering of abused people, but Freud reasoned that regardless of whether someone was actually abused or not, an important issue was how they responded to their suffering. For instance, in his famous case of Dora, Freud discovered that many if not most of her symptoms and complaints were actually derived from copying her father, who often used fake illnesses to escape from family responsibilities.[20] Freud learned from this example that people can fake illnesses and suffering without even knowing that they are faking. Furthermore, a way of manipulating interpersonal relationships is to take on a victim-based status.

As a psychoanalyst, I found that most of my patients saw the world through the lens of victimization, but they were rarely aware of their own perspective even though they used their victimized status to get special treatment from others. We also see this victim-based perspective used in Right-wing politics when the wealthiest and most powerful people claim that they are victims of taxes, government regulations, and political correctness.[21] I have witnessed with my own eyes very wealthy people complain about how they suffer on a daily bases because of their victimization. In fact, Trump often presents himself as a victim of the liberal press, political correctness, the FBI, and his own justice department.

As a main tactic of neoliberalism, the Right has copied the tactics of the Left by claiming victim status, which allows them to demand a reduction of taxes and government spending. Moreover by denying the real existence of racism and sexism in our world, the Right claims that the real victims are rich white males, and from a certain perspective, they are right because as women and people of color gain more power and rights, white males do lose some of their previous privilege and power.

Even if some white men are suffering, the use of victim identity and identification serves to enact the pleasure principle and unconscious primary processes by creating a situation where the aggression of the victim is seen as justified, and irrational emotions are used to create group solidarity. It is important to point out that the Right-wing backlash against global progressive and universal human rights engages in a mirroring relationship with Left-wing identity politics.

I want to stress here that Left-wing, minority-based social movements are necessary for global progress, but they can often become counter-productive when they fixate on their victim status, and they split the world into a good us and an evil other. Once this splitting occurs, repressed aggression can be projected onto the other, which only makes the situation worse. For instance, I recently was part of an online discussion about the role of teacher neutrality in higher education. One of the online discussants argued that neutrality is only a cover for white privilege, and people of color do not have the opportunity to pretend to be neutral. When someone asked her a question about her rejection of impartiality, she then said that the person should remain silent because only people of color should be allowed to talk about oppression. Each time someone tried to move the discussion to a different subject, they were aggressively attacked for being insensitive and a product of white supremacy.

It is interesting that the topic was teacher neutrality because I have been arguing that an essential part of global progress has been the use of neutrality in law and science. In fact, we can see the reality principle as a principle of neutrality, which is itself related to the neutrality of the analyst in the analytic process. Unfortunately, many people now see the very idea of neutrality as a hidden bias created by privileged European white males, and they may be correct about the origin of neutrality, but that does not mean that it cannot be used as a tool for equal justice.

As Pinker documents, the world is becoming more just and equal, but there is still a long way to go, and every movement of progress encounters resistances and regressions. However, one reason why it is important to tell this story of global improvement is that many people believe that we cannot fix any of our problems because they have internalized a Right-wing attack on government. Furthermore, we have to examine what it means that this progress has occurred even without most people knowing that it has happened or understanding the reasons for its occurrence.

Social Practice

One would think that if the greatest achievement ever in human history happened, people would know about it, and they would understand how it happened. Yet, in the case of our global progress, the results have been largely ignored, and so we have to ask how is this possible? One answer to this question relates to the reality principle and the idea that the impartial judge of empirical evidence has to erase his or her own interests and prejudices. In this structure, one must give preference to the responses of reality as one submits to a shared system of social practices embodied in social institutions. From this perspective, the opinion of the isolated ego or person is not what matters; in fact, one must try to erase one's own self in the effort to be impartial. Furthermore, when institutions are shaped by transparent, rational principles and processes, they can function without much individual understanding of how the system works.

Although we are used to thinking that all social actions and ideals are located in the minds of individual people, what happens in reality is that cultural ideas and ideals get embodied in particular practices that transcend the minds of individuals, and here we see the limits of neuroscience and evolutionary psychology. Since you cannot detect a social institution in a brain scan, the new brain sciences often fail to understand how global progress works.[22]

A reasonable question to ask is that if our global institutions work without our awareness, why do we have to learn about them? My first response is that we have to continue to grow and expand this progress, and part of this process revolves around defending globalism against its detractors and enemies. Interestingly, in the United States, there really is no political party representing globalization. The Right often attacks globalization because it undermines national interests, while the Left sees globalization as a cause for lost jobs and economic decline. The reality of the situation is that for most people in the world, globalization has been a great benefit that has increased lifespans, wealth, health, education, rights, and freedom. If you could pick any time in the history of the world to be born, and you did not know where you would end up, today is the best day ever, and tomorrow will be even better.

Of course many academic thinkers hate this idea because it goes against everything they have been taught to believe. Moreover, there are really grave threats to humanity, like climate change and genetic manipulation, but the only way we are going to be able to deal with these problems is if we have faith in the human ability to progress. Paradoxically, the negative attitude on the academic Left concerning global progress inadvertently repeats the Right-wing message that government is the problem and not the solution.

If we dive down and look at the inventions and businesses that have helped to create increased global prosperity and the biggest reduction in poverty ever, we find that most if not all of these companies received financial support from public government.[23] Not only have most medical and pharmaceutical products been supported by government funding, but even companies like Tesla and Apple have relied on generous public support. This combination of business and government means that the

Right is wrong for demonizing public institutions and the Left is wrong for rejecting capitalism. What we need is a fair and transparent combination of the two to help increase global progress.

NOTES

1. Glassner, Barry. *The Culture of Fear: Why Americans Are Afraid of the Wrong Things: Crime, Drugs, Minorities, Teen Moms, Killer Kids, Muta.* Basic Books, 2010.
2. Freud, Sigmund. "'A child is being beaten' a contribution to the study of the origin of sexual perversions." *The Standard Edition of the Complete Psychological Works of Sigmund Freud, Volume XVII (1917–1919): An Infantile Neurosis and Other Works.* 1955. 175–204.
3. Ropeik, David. "The consequences of fear: Our modern world is a risky place and evokes many well-founded fears. But these fears themselves create a new risk for our health and well-being that needs to be addressed." *EMBO Reports* 5.1S (2004): S56–S60.
4. Fromm, Erich. *Escape from Freedom.* Macmillan, 1994.
5. Samuels, Robert. *Psychoanalyzing the Left and Right After Donald Trump: Conservatism, Liberalism, and Neoliberal Populisms.* Springer, 2016.
6. Bloom, Paul. *Against Empathy: The Case for Rational Compassion.* Random House, 2017.
7. Kohut, Heinz and Charles B. Strozier. *Self Psychology and the Humanities: Reflections on a New Psychoanalytic Approach.* New York: W. W. Norton, 1985.
8. Kahneman, Daniel and Patrick Egan. *Thinking, Fast and Slow.* Vol. 1. New York: Farrar, Straus and Giroux, 2011.
9. Samuels, Robert. *Psychoanalyzing the Politics of the New Brain Sciences.* Springer, 2017.
10. Marcuse, Herbert. *Eros and Civilization.* Routledge, 2012.
11. Shakespeare, William. *The New Cambridge Shakespeare: Hamlet, Prince of Denmark.* Ed. Philip Edwards. Cambridge University Press, 2003.
12. Žižek, Slavoj. *The Sublime Object of Ideology.* Verso, 1989.
13. Lacan, *Four*, 49.
14. Kalinich, Lila J. and Stuart W. Taylor, eds. *The Dead Father: A Psychoanalytic Inquiry.* Routledge, 2008.
15. Miller, Jacques-Alain, Paul Verhaeghe, and Ellie Ragland. *Jacques Lacan and the Other Side of Psychoanalysis: Reflections on Seminar XVII, sic vi.* Vol. 6. Duke University Press, 2006.
16. Pinker himself is prone to dismiss or attach all social movements as being based on identity politics.

17. Zinn, Howard. *A People's History of the United States: 1492-Present.* Routledge, 2015.
18. Cole, Alyson Manda. *The Cult of True Victimhood: From the War on Welfare to the War on Terror.* Stanford University Press, 2007.
19. Schimek, Jean G. "Fact and fantasy in the seduction theory: A historical review." *Journal of the American Psychoanalytic Association* 35.4 (1987): 937–965.
20. Freud, Sigmund. *Dora: An Analysis of a Case of Hysteria.* Simon and Schuster, 1997.
21. Frank, Thomas. *Pity the Billionaire: The Hard-Times Swindle and the Unlikely Comeback of the Right.* Macmillan, 2012.
22. Samuels, Robert. *Psychoanalyzing the Politics of the New Brain Sciences.* Springer, 2017.
23. Mazzucato, Mariana. "The entrepreneurial state." *Soundings* 49.49 (2011): 131–142.

CHAPTER 7

Conclusion: Progress and Its Discontents

Abstract The final chapter looks at Yuval Harari's *21 Lessons for the 21st Century* to examine why liberal academic culture often rejects global progress and focuses on negative portrayals of the world. By using Freud's fundamental concepts to analyze Harari's work, I provide a model for psychoanalytic cultural criticism. The goal then of this work is to show that psychoanalysis is not only still relevant today, but in actuality, Freud's theories and practices have never been more essential for understanding and changing ourselves and the world around us.

Keywords Yuval Harari · Liberalism · Academic culture · Criticism · Freud

I want to end this book by examining a series of difficult global problems brought up in Yuval Harari's book *21 Lessons for the 21st Century*.[1] I turn to this book because Harari's work is an interesting example of the way that liberal academic culture often denies global progress. For example, be begins by presenting a now common perception of the world today: "At the close of the twentieth century it appeared that the great ideological battles between fascism, communism, and liberalism had resulted in the overwhelming victory of liberalism. Democratic politics, human rights, and free-market capitalism seemed destined to conquer the entire world. But as usual, history took an unexpected turn, and after fascism and communism collapsed, now liberalism is in trouble" (xvi).

An important aspect of this passage is that it begins by telling the story of global progress, but then it focuses on current resistances to this development. Although, it is not my intention to deny the very real threats facing our world today, the emphasis on the negative represents a distortion of reality that we will see throughout his work.

Just as the media and politicians represent the most negative aspects of the world in order to gain attention, academic thinkers and writers are often trained to focus on the negative. Part of this may be due to their training in critical analysis, but another part may relate to the way that liberal culture at times finds pleasure in the suffering of others.[2] While movies and television programs turn tragedy into comedy and entertainment, liberal academic culture often feeds off the ability to enact the pleasure principle through the process of pointing to a problem and then removing the audience and the analyst from any direct responsibility.

We see a strong example of the way that attention is generated through the presentation of the negative in the following passage: "The merger of infotech and biotech might soon push billions of humans out of the job market and undermine both liberty and equality. Big Data algorithms might create digital dictatorships in which all power is concentrated in the hands of a tiny elite while most people suffer not from exploitation but from something far worse—irrelevance" (xvi). Once again, while I am not denying that some of these horrible things may happen, we have to ask the psychoanalytic question of what pleasure does Harari get from painting such a horrific view of the future?

In returning to the analytic concept of masochistic fantasy, we can see that by focusing on the negative, Harari is able to take on the position of the helpless victim who is innocent and pure, and who sees evil in the external world. Like an obsessional who imagines the worst so that when it does not happen, he feels better, contemporary liberal academic culture tends to present a highly negative view of the world, and this view is often passed down to students. As Harari admits, one reason why academic thinkers and writers may be so negative is that they want to counter-balance what they see as the overly optimistic portrayal of the world outside of the academic world: "The book does not attempt to cover all the impacts of the new technologies. In particular, though technology holds many wonderful promises, my intention here is to highlight mainly its threats and dangers. Since the corporations and entrepreneurs who lead the technological revolution naturally tend to sing the praises of their creations, it falls to sociologists, philosophers, and historians such as myself to sound the alarm and explain all the ways things can go terribly wrong" (xvii). The problem with this concentration on threats and dangers is that it blinds us from seeing the real achievements in global progress, and this failure to to se the positive can cause us to lose faith in our ability to deal collectively with any future problem. It is as if we are winning a game, but because we think we are losing, we have no confidence in our ability to continue to win or to deal with adversity. After all, how will we be able to confront all of the horrible things Harari highlights if we do not know that we have been successful in improving the world?[3]

Harari's rhetoric thus places him and us in a victimized position because we are told about all of these horrible things that are or will be happening as we are also robbed of our belief in our ability to change things. Like the helpless victim watching a scene of abuse, our pleasure comes from our distance from the action. As I have discussed in my analysis of Freud's theory of beating fantasies, the first level of the fantasy is the claim that a group of unknown children are being beaten by an unknown man, and the reporter of the fantasy has been reduced to being a passive viewer of the suffering.[4] Freud adds that this first level of fantasy is mediated by a second fantasy where it is the reporter of the fantasy who is now being beaten by a father. In the case of Harari, we see this portrayal of victimization in the following passage: "Should I speak my mind openly and risk that my words might be taken out of context and used to justify burgeoning autocracies? Or should I censor myself? It is a mark of illiberal regimes that they make free speech more difficult even outside their borders. Due to the spread of such regimes, it is becoming increasingly dangerous to think critically about the future of our species" (xix). Here we find a hysterical victim identification as the mere act of writing a book is compared to being censored and possibly imprisoned in an oppressive regime. By taking on the position of being a threatened victim, Harari is able to accomplish the goal of the pleasure principle to avoid all shame, guilt, and responsibility because the victim should never be criticized.[5]

The reason why I am focusing on this work is that is reveals an important obstacle to global progress, which is paradoxically liberal academic culture. Although you would think that liberals would love to tell the story of liberalism's success, Harari's rhetoric shows why liberals feels so ambivalent about their own culture and history: "The liberal story celebrates the value and power of liberty. It says that for thousands of years humankind lived under oppressive regimes that allowed people few political rights, economic opportunities, or personal liberties, and which heavily restricted the movements of individuals, ideas, and goods. But people fought for their freedom, and step by step, liberty gained ground. Democratic regimes took the place of brutal dictatorships. Free enterprise overcame economic restrictions. People learned to think for themselves and follow their hearts instead of blindly obeying bigoted priests and hidebound traditions. Open roads, wide bridges, and bustling airports replaced walls, moats, and barbed-wire fences" (3). In many ways, this narrative represents the truth of global progress, and yet Harari will soon turn on this story in an effort to warn us of all the things that can go wrong. Perhaps his ambivalence is derived from an underlying desire to have an ideal world without conflict, and so any problem is experienced as a failure of the whole project. However, by letting the perfect be the enemy of the good, liberal culture turns on itself and undermines its own success.

A good example of his ambivalent relation to liberalism is found in his description of the current world order: "Much of our planet is dominated by tyrants, and even in the most liberal countries many citizens suffer from poverty, violence, and oppression. But at least we know what we need to do in order to overcome these problems: give people more liberty. We need to protect human rights, grant everybody the vote, establish free markets, and let individuals, ideas, and goods move throughout the world as easily as possible. According to this liberal panacea—accepted, in slight variations, by George W. Bush and Barack Obama alike—if we just continue to liberalize and globalize our political and economic systems, we will produce peace and prosperity for all" (4). I think a problem with this passage is that it confuses two different versions of liberalism. One version concerns the role played by reason, democracy, and science since the Enlightenment, and the other is the type of liberal culture I have been critiquing. In the first form of liberalism, the reality principle is used in science and democracy to deal with problems in an open and truthful manner, while in the second form of liberalism, people deny reality and use the primary processes in the unconscious to achieve the aims of the pleasure principle. Part of this second form involves turning all suffering into a form of pleasure as one signals one's virtue through one's outrage regarding the failures of the world to live up to one's utopian desires.

Like many people on the political Left, Harari points to the global financial crisis of 2008 to show why liberal global progress has failed: "However, since the global financial crisis of 2008 people all over the world have become increasingly disillusioned with the liberal story. Walls and firewalls are back in vogue. Resistance to immigration and to trade agreements is mounting. Ostensibly democratic governments undermine the independence of the judiciary system, restrict the freedom of the press, and portray any opposition as treason. Strongmen in countries such as Turkey and Russia experiment with new types of illiberal democracies and outright dictatorships. Today, few would confidently declare that the Chinese Communist Party is on the wrong side of history" (4). While all of the problems Harari lists are real, what cannot be denied is that we continue to see people's lives on average getting better around the world. Perhaps one cause for the focus on the negative is that some of the progress made in the "non-developed world" has come at the expense of a loss of economic opportunity for some people in the "developed world."6 Thus as millions of people are brought out of dire poverty in China, India, and Africa, some jobs have disappeared in the United States and some European countries. In fact, the Right-wing backlash in America and England can be in part due to the unequal effects of economic globalization. However, by blaming all of the economic problems on immigration, the Right blinds us from the reality of automation and the global labor and production system.

Harari himself does not see how globalization continues to be a net benefit to the world, and instead he emphasizes the Right-wing backlash to this system: "The year 2016—marked by the Brexit vote in Britain and the rise of Donald Trump in the United States—signified the moment when this tidal wave of disillusionment reached the core liberal states of Western Europe and North America. Whereas a few years ago Americans and Europeans were still trying to liberalize Iraq and Libya at gunpoint, many people in Kentucky and Yorkshire now have come to see the liberal vision as either undesirable or unattainable. Some discovered a liking for the old hierarchical world, and they just don't want to give up their racial, national, or gendered privileges. Others have concluded (rightly or wrongly) that liberalization and globalization are a huge racket empowering a tiny elite at the expense of the masses" (5). In repeating the Right-wing narrative about globalization, Harari unintentionally reveals how contemporary liberals often buy into the ideology they attack. For instance in the 2016 US presidential election, Hilary Clinton and Bernie Sanders echoed Trump's attack on globalization: the only difference was they did not couple this criticism with an attack on immigrants. Instead, they focused their hatred on Trump and the global elites.

The sad truth of the matter is that very few politicians understand or recognize the benefits of globalization for the world and that is why it is so important to try to have a fact-based discussion about public policy and the state of the world today. Just as psychoanalysis tries to get us to replace the pleasure principle, unconscious primary process, and transference with the reality principle, we have to find a way to base political decisions on empirical evidence and not ideology or personal self-interest. Part of this process requires mourning the lost of the old patriarchal order, which was structured by a set of stable prejudices and social hierarchies. In fact, if we want to understand what global progress is fighting against, we can look at Aristotle's outline of the premodern social order:

> for the soul rules the body with a despotical rule, whereas the intellect rules the appetites with a constitutional and royal rule. And it is clear that the rule of the soul over the body, and of the mind and the rational element over the passionate, is natural and expedient; whereas the equality of the two or the rule of the inferior is always hurtful. The same holds good of animals in relation to men; for tame animals have a better nature than wild, and all tame animals are better off when they are ruled by man; for then they are preserved. Again, the male is by nature superior, and the female inferior; and the one rules, and the other is ruled; this principle, of necessity, extends to all mankind. (Book 1, part V)[7]

Aristotle describes here a social system that is structured by a series of reinforcing hierarchies and analogies that are presented as being inevitable because they are seen as being natural and efficient: according to this logic, just as it is natural for the master to rule over the slave, it is natural for males to dominate females, for humans to rule over animals, and for the mind to rule over the body.[8] It is precisely this logic and social order that globalization has been overturning, and this social revolution has not been the result of natural or divine order; instead, people working together have knowingly and unknowingly created a world that is more just and fair. It seems unlikely that this process will be reversed because just as one cannot completely erase a memory, it is hard to get rid of a new idea or technology once it has been released into the world.

From a psychoanalytic perspective, we can say that the system of reinforcing hierarchies and oppositions presented by Aristotle point to the way that a linguistic system of substitutions and displacements is projected onto the world and is then seen as being natural. In the same way that the unconscious primary processes confuse thoughts with perceptions, premodern culture is founded on an artificial symbolic system that is confused with natural order. Freud calls this projection of ideas into the external world, "the omnipotence of thoughts," and he argues that one of the roles of science in the form of the reality principle is to teach us to give up on the omnipotence of our own thinking.[9]

A defining aspect of modernity has been the denaturalization of the social order, and this change in perspective has empowered people to believe that they can make the social world more just and fair. Paradoxically, by giving up on the ultimate power of our thoughts, we have been able to use necessary but impossible ideals to transform the world. Even though we can never be completely impartial or logical, the process of striving to attain these ideal views has created social institutions and practices leading to global progress.

Since our global advancement has not moved in a straight line and has not always been visible, we often take for granted our progress as we concentrate on the resistances to positive social change. Harari falls victim to this tendency to repress the true movement of history: "By the early 1990s, thinkers and politicians alike hailed 'the End of History,' confidently asserting that all the big political and economic questions of the past had been settled and that the refurbished liberal package of democracy, human rights, free markets, and government welfare services remained the only game in town. This package seemed destined to spread around the whole world, overcome all obstacles, erase all national borders, and turn humankind into one free global community. But history has not ended, and following the Franz Ferdinand moment, the Hitler moment, and the Che Guevara moment, we now find ourselves in the Trump moment. This time, however, the liberal story is not faced by a coherent ideological opponent like imperialism, fascism, or communism. The Trump moment is far more nihilistic" (11). Since human progress does not fallow a linear path and is not guided by a divine or natural force, there are always regressions and resistance, but one cannot deny that over the last 150 years, global lifespans have doubled, and this extension of life must be seen as an ultimate sign of progress. In fact, one reason why Trump appears to be so threatening and depressing is that his words and policies stand in such contrast with the path of human progress. If the exception proves the rule, we should see our outrage with Trump as evidence that he is a horrible exception proving the rule of global progress.

What is so curious about Harari's argument is that he does not believe that liberal democracy can still deal with the problems facing the world today: "But liberalism has no obvious answers to the biggest problems we face: ecological collapse and technological disruption. Liberalism traditionally relied on economic growth to magically solve difficult social and political conflicts" (16). What Harari gets wrong here is his failure to recognize that modern globalization has relied on a balance among three different social systems: science, democracy, and capitalism. Although many free market libertarians now only focus on the role played by capitalism, it was the roles played by democratic law and scientific discovery that helped to pave the way for global progress; it is therefore difficult to see why these modern systems cannot continue to guide the world to a better social system.

However, in seeing the world from the perspective of potential catastrophes, the paranoid mind sees signs everywhere of our impending doom: "The liberal story and the logic of free-market capitalism encourage people to have grand expectations. During the latter part of the twentieth century, each generation—whether in Houston, Shanghai, Istanbul, or São Paulo—enjoyed better education, superior healthcare and larger incomes than the one that came before it. In coming decades, however, owing to a combination of technological disruption and ecological meltdown, the younger generation might be lucky to simply stay in place" (16). One way of understanding this lost faith in global progress is through Freud's theory that in states of anxiety, we revert to the primary processes, which allows us to make mental connections between things that are not naturally connected. What then is the cause of Harari's and other contemporary liberal thinkers' anxieties is that that we are witnessing a world of unprecedented technological change that leaves us in a state of uncertainty: "Since the beginning of the Industrial Revolution, for every job lost to a machine at least one new job was created, and the average standard of living has increased dramatically. Yet there are good reasons to think that this time it is different and that machine learning will be a real game changer" (19). While we do not know if this fear of automation replacing most jobs will occur, presently, automation and other new technologies have increased global well-being, and yet, Harari warns that we should imagine the worst: "The potential social and political disruptions are so alarming that even if the probability of systemic mass unemployment is low, we should take it very seriously" (33). Although there is nothing bad about planning for future problems, we need to base our public policies and our views of the world on facts and not projected fears.

It is very telling that Harari relies on evolutionary psychology in order to define how feelings are derived and the ways these feelings may affect our views of the world around us: "Rather, feelings are biochemical mechanisms that all mammals and birds use in order to quickly calculate probabilities of survival and reproduction. Feelings aren't based on intuition, inspiration, or freedom—they are based on calculation. When a monkey, mouse, or human sees a snake, fear arises because millions of neurons in the brain swiftly calculate the relevant data and conclude that the probability of death is high. Feelings of sexual attraction arise when other biochemical algorithms calculate that a nearby individual offers a high probability of successful mating, social bonding, or some other coveted goal. Moral feelings such as outrage, guilt, or forgiveness derive from neural mechanisms that evolved to enable group cooperation. All these biochemical algorithms were honed through millions of years of evolution" (47). From a psychoanalytic perspective, what is wrong about this theory is that it does not account for the way that the pleasure principle, the primary processes, and transference replace our natural responses derived from natural selection with social and psychological reactions. Humans thus have a fear of the future not because they are simply responding to mental programs inherited from biology; rather, our responses are filtered through social and unconscious mechanisms. For example, Harari's fear of the future may activate biological systems that generate anxiety in the face of uncertainty, but the act of understanding the world as a cause of anxiety is based on personal and social associations. It is therefore necessary to trace these associations and map out how they distort reality, and I hope that my reading of Harari's work has helped to provide a model for this process of cultural free association.

THE FUTURE OF PROGRESS

One of the paradoxes revealed in this book is that global progress is perhaps the greatest human achievement, but very few people know that it has been happening, and even fewer people understand why it has happened. If reason in law and science, in the form of the reality principle, has been the driving force, then we must affirm that reason works best when it is embodied in particular social practices and institutions. In fact, a major part of the reality principle and science for Freud is the giving up of the power of our own thoughts, and this process of self-effacement means that it is not our individual thinking that fuels progress.

A conclusion that we can draw from the role of the reality principle in global progress is the need to create better social practices and institutions while we downplay the importance of individual participation. The result of this focus on collective behavior beyond individual subjectivity could mean a greater reliance on rational technological programs in the future. After all, if we turn to self-driving cars because they make fewer mental errors compared to humans, then why do we not turn most of our political decisions over to computers programs to apply the reality principle and science to every public policy decision? For many people, this move is very threatening, but if we really want our politics to be based on reason and not ideology and special interest, then we need to consider the use of new technologies in automating our social decisions. Since the unconscious can be considered to be a machine that satisfies desire through hallucination and imagination, we may need to short-circuit this internal machine by programming better external machines.

NOTES

1. Harari, Yuval Noah. *21 Lessons for the 21st Century*. Random House, 2018.
2. Mann, Paul. *Masocriticism*. SUNY Press, 1999.
3. Ehring, Thomas and Edward R. Watkins. "Repetitive negative thinking as a transdiagnostic process." *International Journal of Cognitive Therapy* 1.3 (2008): 192–205.
4. Freud, Sigmund. "'A child is being beaten' a contribution to the study of the origin of sexual perversions." *The Standard Edition of the Complete Psychological Works of Sigmund Freud, Volume XVII (1917–1919): An Infantile Neurosis and Other Works*. 1955. 175–204.
5. Cole, Alyson Manda. *The Cult of True Victimhood: From the War on Welfare to the War on Terror*. Stanford University Press, 2007.
6. Pinker, Steven. *Enlightenment Now: The Case for Reason, Science, Humanism, and Progress*. Penguin Books, 2019.
7. Barnes, Jonathan, ed. *The Cambridge Companion to Aristotle*. Cambridge University Press, 1995.
8. Nietzsche argues that Aristotle simply describes his traits as ideal, and then he defines the opposite of his traits as debased. Nietzsche, Friedrich Wilhelm, and Reginald John Hollingdale. *On the Genealogy of Morals*. Vintage, 1989.
9. Freud, Sigmund. *Totem and Taboo: Some Points of Agreement Between the Mental Lives of Savages and Nuerotics*. Routledge, 2013.

INDEX

CPSIA information can be obtained
at www.ICGtesting.com
Printed in the USA
LVHW081100180819
628039LV00014B/691/P